the ANIMAL SPEAK workbook

Other Books by Ted Andrews

Animal Speak
Animal Wise
Crystal Balls & Crystal Bowls
Dream Alchemy
Enchantment of the Faerie Realm
The Healer's Manual
How to Heal with Color
How to Meet and Work with Spirit Guides
How to See and Read the Aura
How to Uncover Your Past Lives
Nature Speak
Psychic Protection
The Sacred Power in Your Name
Sacred Sounds
Simplified Qabala Magic

TED ANDREWS

the ANIMAL SPEAK workbook

LLEWELLYN
WOODBURY, MINNESOTA

Dragonhawk Publishing

Note: The text for this edition is the originally published work. There are words and phrases included in this text that are outdated and no longer culturally acceptable.

First Printing
Originally published by Dragonhawk Publishing in 2002
First Llewellyn Publications Edition, 2026

Cover design by Shira Atakpu
Cover art by Siolo Thompson

ISBN: 978-0-7387-8346-8

Library of Congress Cataloging-in-Publication Data
On file with the Library of Congress, Catalog Card Number 2002108332.
Copyright is registered with the Library of Congress
Registratrion Number: TX0006066194.

Llewellyn Publications
A Division of Llewellyn Worldwide Ltd.
2143 Wooddale Drive
Woodbury, MN 55125-2989
www.llewellyn.com

Printed in the United States of America

GPSR Representation:
UPI-2M PLUS d.o.o., Medulićeva 20, 10000 Zagreb, Croatia
matt.parsons@upi2mbooks.hr

In loving memory of
Jag,
Ben,
Phoenix
and
Avalon, the white wolf

Table of Contents

If you create a memory,

If you ignite a spark of wonder,

Their hearts will open to Nature... forever.

On July 21, 2002 Phoenix, our red-tailed hawk, died. She inspired wonder and touched the hearts of nearly eight thousand young people. This was her last program. She lives forever in our hearts and we thank her for sharing her life with us.

The Birth of Shenandoah

She would be our first foal. We had bought her mother pregnant, but no one was exactly sure when she had been bred back. Finally all of the signs were there. The birth was imminent. And we were so excited. We began visiting her stall every couple hours, wanting to be there for the event. At one A.M. there was still no change. I made my way back to the house, thinking that we had misread the signs and that tonight wasn't the night at all.

I didn't bother going back to bed. Instead, I lay down on a couch next to a window that looked out at the aviary where we kept Phoenix, our red-tailed hawk and was soon asleep.

"Get up."

I slowly opened my eyes to see Phoenix perched on the back of the couch. It took me a moment before I realized that I must still be asleep.

"It's time."

Then I am walking down my driveway toward the barn. Phoenix is flying from tree to tree ahead of me. I am thrilled to see her fly because in the waking world, she can't. She is permanently injured. As I reach the gate to the paddock, Phoenix swoops down over my head and flies back toward the house.

A large moose walks by me in the paddock. I am so surprised that it is a moment before I realize with certainty that the foal has been born. And with that realization, I wake up.

I go to the bedroom and wake my wife. I tell her that Phoenix has just told me the foal has been born. I grab a flashlight and a cell phone to call her with confirmation from the barn, and I hurry out into the dark.

The moon is bright, and it is about 4:00 A.M. Everything is still and quiet, encloaked in a soft hush. I move quietly into the barn. The mother's stall is in the back. I keep the flashlight low, so as not to startle the horses. I step up to the stall door. Moonlight filters through the back window, illuminating it. The mother is lying against the back wall - asleep. Not far from her in a moonlit glow is a beautiful, healthy foal...

Chapter 1

The Message Bringers

You are driving in your car and a hawk flies in front of you. The crow sitting in the tree seems to be looking right at you. You dream of a lion attacking you. You see yourself becoming a beautiful butterfly in your meditation. The same animal appears every time you walk outside. A part of you knows that these encounters have meaning, but how can you truly come to understand them?

Early shamans were mystics, magicians *and* scientists. They spent time in Nature, studying the animals, learning about them in order to awaken their power more fully and to interpret their messages more accurately. Today we can do this for ourselves, but we must learn to experience animals and Nature in a new way.

Nature is the most powerful realm of magic and spirituality upon the Earth. It is the source of primal energies and great spirits. Within it are found most of life's lessons and most of life's answers. There are teachings about life, death and rebirth. There are teachings of creativity and the development of survival skills, applicable to our modern world. Within Nature are revelations for solving problems and accomplishing tasks that seem impossible. Through Nature we learn respect, nurturing and trust in our perceptions. It is a reminder of our greatest possibilities.

And Nature is speaking to us all of the time. The problem is that most people have forgotten how to listen. We have separated ourselves from Nature. Nature is something to be studied from a distance or solely from books. It is often something to be taken advantage of, and it is often thought to have little significance to the modern world, other than as a realm of recreation. But we are part of Nature. Everything that happens in the natural world has repercussions upon us, and everything that happens to us has repercussions on the natural world. No matter how much we cloak ourselves

Are You Craving Road Kill?

All traditions taught that no animal is any better, any more spiritual than any other animal. Every animal has qualities that are unique, and the animal that has appeared in our life has done so because its qualities will work best for us at that time. In Western society there is a tendency to glamorize certain animals - to think some are more spiritual, powerful and better than others are.

When I teach workshops on animal totems. I ask the participants, "How many of you would like a vulture as a totem?" A few giggles and maybe a single raise of the hand usually follow this. The vulture is not a glamorous animal. It is a magnificent bird though.

Yes, it is the garbage man of the environment. It feeds on the dead. It is a scavenger, but it cleans up the environment. By doing so, it prevents the spread of disease. The vulture has a unique digestive system. It has 40,000 times more resistance to botulism than the human body, which is good, considering what it eats. Its digestive tract elicits a chemical that serves as a bactericide, enabling it to derive nutrition from what it is feeding upon. When vulture shows up in your life, it is not an indication that you will be having cravings for road kill, but you can expect a change in your digestive processes. Foods you didn't like, you may start to like. Foods you used to eat lots of and never have problems may not agree with you anymore.

To the Pueblo people it is a sacred bird of healing, its feathers used in most healing ceremonies for its gentle balancing and curative effects. In Egypt it was associated with the goddess Maat, the goddess of truth. One legend tells of how the Egyptian gods and goddesses evaluate a soul when it has passed from physical life. The individual's actions and behaviors are weighed to determine the life or death of the soul. The Goddess Maat, holding her vulture feather, asks the final question, which determines the ultimate judgment of the soul. Her question is simply, "Is there one who is glad that you lived?" If the answer is yes, her feather is laid in the scale, balancing it in your favor and the soul moves on to the heavens.

The vulture is a bird that is sacred, no matter how unglamorous it might seem. When it comes to spirit animals and totems, we have to get rid of our preconceptions and misconceptions. No animal is any more powerful or spiritual than any other animal. That animal has shown up because it is important to you and your life at this time. Remember that each species has its own unique qualities. An ant may not seem as glamorous as a bear, but an ant is industrious and has a strength that far exceeds its size. Part of working with Nature and animals is to break down outworn perceptions.

in civilization we will always be a part of Nature.

When we chose to live and grow upon the Earth, we were anointed with certain responsibilities. One of these was to be a *Steward of the Earth.* Stewards are guardians, caretakers, overseers and coworkers. Stewardship in business was often a work-study type of program with a unique set of responsibilities. It often involved living with, working along side of and overseeing the activities of others. It is a role of caring, protection and partnership.

We must take back upon ourselves the innate responsibility as Stewards of the Earth. This means we must develop a new relationship with the Earth and form a new perspective of our relationship to its creatures. Among the Native Americans is the core belief that they are brothers and sisters to everything in Nature. They have always been stewards, as have been many indigenous peoples. Animals are their companions, allies, teachers, guardians, spirit messengers and even younger siblings needing protection at times. As such, they are given the respect that one gives to any member of the human family.

For many in today's modern world this is difficult to accept, especially in our scientific and rational society. There was a time though when each of us knew this truth in our hearts. As children we were often more aware than was ever acknowledged. We knew that animals spoke and trees whispered. We knew there was wisdom and magic throughout the natural world. Sadly, most people were eventually socialized, shamed, and even educated out of this inner knowing. But it is never truly lost.

In our modern world it is easy to get so wrapped up in fulfilling our daily obligations and responsibilities that we forget that we can starve as much from a lack of wonder as we can from a lack of food. If only for this reason, it is important to reconnect with Nature – to find what has been lost. Nature – and animals in particular – awaken our sense of wonder. And this wonder keeps our inner magic alive and our spirit strong. Through this workbook, you will learn to experience Nature and animals in a fresh way. You will learn to see and experience with a child's eyes. And in the process you will find that part of you, which is still magical, mysterious and filled with wonder.

Six Steps to Changing

Shamanism is an experiential growth process. It involves becoming the master of your own initiation, your own spiritual path. The individual is able to learn from all life forms – especially the animals. Pursuing our spiritual quest and unfolding our innate powers through reconnecting with Nature begins with changing our perspective about Nature and animals. We must overcome preconceived notions and limitations.

1 **Involve yourself with some aspect of Nature more personally.** A recent survey stated that the average person in the US spends less than an hour a week outdoors and most of this is time spent going to and from cars. We cannot expect to truly open communication with the natural world if we do not spend some quality time in it. Plant a garden. Allow an area of your yard to grow wild so that the wildlife can take up residence within it. Become an amateur naturalist. Do some bird watching. Create a pond. Seek out marshlands. Take night hikes. Try to identify birds by their calls. Try to identify trees by their leaves. Volunteer and support nature, centers, zoos and other environmental organizations. Above all, study animals and all of Nature.

2 **Imagine the animals as younger brothers or sisters.** Just like humans, some animals need more care, protection and guidance than others do. Begin imagining and looking upon every animal as a younger sibling or as a favorite pet for whom you have a deep love and respect. See every animal as you would your pet.

Earlier this spring, my wife and I rescued a red-tailed hawk with a head injury. She recovered enough to be released back into the wild. For several weeks, she remained close by, neither hunting nor flying far. We were leaving some food out for her, because she didn't seem to be hunting. We began to fear that we released her too soon. Then she began to disappear for days at a time. Now she has learned to live on her own. When she returns, it is just to let us know that she is doing fine. She is our wild, pet hawk. She is truly a friend, a member of our family, who pays us wonderful visits from time to time.

3 **Imagine the animals having cognitive thought processes, even if you don't understand them.** Humans have many varying levels of mental ability – some finely developed and some even challenged, but this does not prevent us from giving them the respect due to them. The same holds true for animals.

Your Perspective

The ability to love and respect another (human or animal) should never be determined by that person or animal's degree of intelligence or seeming lack of it. Try thinking of them as you would a foreigner who can not speak your language and who simply speaks in a language you don't understand yet. In time, you will realize that animals have varying levels of emotion and even cognitive processes – just like humans.

4 **Listen for and acknowledge Nature's daily greetings to you.** When you are outside, if only for a few moments, pay attention to what stands out for you. It may be a crow cawing to you. It may be a fragrance from a tree. Nature usually greets us in some way every time we step outside. The more you acknowledge it, the stronger the greetings become. If the fragrance of a tree or flower catches your attention, greet it. If a bird speaks as you step out, mimic its greeting back to it. If a crow caws, caw back. If you are uncomfortable doing this, then just say something like, "Hello, friend crow."

5 **Read animal tales and myths from different traditions and countries.** By reading animal tales and myths from different parts of the world, three things will happen. First, you will begin to recognize common teaching about the animals. Second you will begin to see some of the spiritual qualities and archetypal energies associated with the animal. Third, you build a bridge between your world the more subtle realms of life – between the human world and the animal world.

In today's world animal images/encounters and their meaning to our reality have grown stale. They have lost their ability to touch each of us uniquely. Tales and myths help restore our connection and open us to a more personal epiphany with Nature. Animal tales help us to unfold our intuition, creativity, and imagination. They become doorways and we can visit the heavens and the underworld through them.

6 **Embrace your role as Steward of the Earth.** We are related to everything in Nature, and we must begin to imagine, think and act as if we understand that relationship. If we persist in this effort, the doors of our awareness reopen. We begin to understand our true relationship to the animal world. We are no longer at the top of the food chain. Instead we are the stewards. Just as we may have had to watch over younger brothers and sisters, so too must we do so with the animal world. For they are our brothers and sisters as well.

Spirit Animals and Totems

A totem is any natural object, being or animal with which we feel closely associated and whose phenomena and energy are related to our life in some way. Some totems reflect energies operating for only short periods of time. Others remain with us from birth, through death and beyond. They are symbols and forces for integration, expression and transformation.

A totem is anything of the natural world that has significance for us. It can be a stone, a tree, a flower, a landscape or an animal. Trees can whisper and stones can speak. We are focusing upon animal totems and messengers in this book, but we should remember that spirit messages do not always come through the animal kingdom. Of all totem types, animal images and encounters are often the most valid signposts within our life. Because of this, I will use the term totem to refer to animal totems, animal spirits and/or animals synonymously throughout the book.

Animal totems are messengers, communicating to us about our lives and about us. Discovering the meanings of the messages they bring is sometimes difficult, but there is no doubt that animal encounters – whether in dreams, waking life or meditation - stimulate some primordial part of our imagination. They help liberate the mind, opening us to possibilities beyond our daily routines.

There are five main types of totems we are all likely to have. There is some variation depending upon the particular tradition, and some of the roles overlap. For example, a power animal may also be a protector and a message bringer. We can also have several animals in each of these categories.

Message Bringers

These are often animals whose appearance provides guidance in our life. They bring direction to us about situations, choices, decisions and activities we are involved in. Their presence is often temporary. A study of their characteristics and behaviors provide clues and insight as to what our behaviors and actions should be in situations around us. When we have a problem, learning to ask for guidance and then taking a nature walk to get the message is one of the best ways of finding answers.

Personal Power Animals

Power totems are animals that are with us throughout our life or through major periods within our life. They are message bringers, protectors, teachers and healers. Different traditions disagree about how many power animals we have. It can vary, each animal working and helping us in different areas of our life. For example, one of my totems is the red-tailed hawk. I have worked hands on with hawks and other birds of prey for many years, and I have also worked spiritually with them for many years. Hawk has helped me to develop and focus my spiritual / psychic vision. It has taught me patience and it serves as a messenger to warn me of the ease or difficulty of the path ahead of me. But it is not my only power animal.

Protectors

Protectors are often power animals, but these are animals that give us extra strength and energy, often without our realizing it at the moment. They alert us to trouble. They often appear in dreams of conflict to let us know what qualities to draw on to handle the conflicts in our life. Many people wrongly assume that protectors are always big and ferocious animals. They can be, but every animal has its own unique defense strategies and abilities. While dragons are powerful protectors for many aspects of my life, the opossum also serves as a protector for me. When it appears in my life, it warns me that things and people around me are not what they seem to be. Opossum warns me to be careful of my own words and actions, that I may need to "play possum" in some situations.

Teachers

All animals that come to us are teachers. They teach us about our own potentials, about energies at play within our life and about our spiritual path in this life. We can learn something from every animal, but those who appear regularly have something special to teach us. They also serve as spiritual guides for us, leading us and helping us in sacred quests and journeys. Often animals that appear regularly in our dreams are teaching totems. They are guides into and out of the dream world and the underworld. Take a look at the animals that are living in the same environment in which you are living. These animals are usually doing so quite successfully. They can teach us to live more successfully within that same environment – whether it is the home, work, school or some other kind of environment.

Healing Animals

These animals provide us with energy and guidance in regards to healing others or ourselves. Many animals have unique resistance to certain diseases and drawing upon that animal's energy helps us be more resistant to it as well. Some animals are archetypal symbols of healing. The snake is one such animal. It sheds the old skin and moves into the new. It is a symbol of leaving the old behind for the new. As a symbol of transformation, meditating and focusing on the snake during times of illness will help accelerate the healing process. Animals that appear to us at times of illness, provide clues as to the best way to focus our healing energies.

Discover Your Animal

There are many ways of determining what your animal spirits and totems are. Some methods are ritualistic and complicated, but others are quite simple. It is not as difficult or mysterious as some may have you think. And keep in mind that we will always have more than one totem or messenger because nothing exists alone in Nature. We may have some that are with us throughout our lives. Others will show up at different times to help us solve problems, accomplish tasks, aid in healing or for other functions discussed earlier. With just a little observation and introspection, we can begin to recognize our totems.

What animal(s) were you most drawn to or interested in as a child?

An old occult axiom teaches, "Like attracts like." Looking toward the animals we were drawn to as children often points us to our power animals. If you have children of your own, what animal(s) is he or she most interested in? If it is more than one child, it is usually a different animal. I have a nephew who was absolutely fascinated by insects as a child, and I have a niece who only wanted to see the elephants when taken to the zoo. By studying that animal the child is drawn to, you can get a new perspective on your child. It provides a way of understanding and relating to the unique individuality of that child. The same holds true for us.

What animal(s) are you most drawn to or fascinated by right now?

At every major phase within our life, our power animals shift. New messengers come in and others step aside. No one animal can be everything for us. Yes, there is usually one or two that we can always go to for guidance, but they will often send to us that animal that more clearly and appropriately can help us at that time.

Do you dream of certain animals?

Every tradition recognized that the dream world was just as real and important as our waking world. Animal encounters in dreams should be treated just as you would an unusual encounter with the animal in the waking. In dreams we can encounter any kind of animal. We are not limited to geographical boundaries, thus making any animal of the world a possible totem. The nice thing about dream animals is that by looking at the other elements in the dream (who else is in it and where it takes place, etc.) we have clues as to where this animal's energies and wisdom should be applied in our waking life.

What animal appears when you start something new?

When I teach a new subject, I look to see what animal appears as guide for me with that subject. I have found that when I travel to teach in new areas, new animals show up, providing clues as to how the trip will be. On my first major

Messengers and Totems

teaching tour of the Midwest I encountered three pheasants on the first day of the trip. On each occasion, the pheasant flew in front of the car. The Midwest has been one of my most popular and successful areas to teach in and everytime in the past ten years when I do a major tour of the Midwest, the pheasant appears early on.

Every part of the country in which I teach has had its own unique animal encounters for me, reflecting the energies of the events. In the Southwest, coyote appears. In the Northwest, it is quail. In the East it is the hawk and the heron. In many cases, each state has a particular animal that shows up for me within an hour of arriving. For example, Colorado is usually the red fox and Misouri is the turtle. The encounters always reflect the energy of that trip and help me know how to adjust my teaching for the greatest success of the events.

When you start something new, pay attention to the animal that seems to be appearing in your life. It will guide you with the tasks at hand. The same holds true for any new problem or issue that arises.

What animal most frightens you or makes you feel uncomfortable?

Animals that we respond to with strong emotions are usually some of our most important totems. They are often our power animals. They are helpers and messengers about major issues reoccurring within our life. We will explore them in the exercise at the end of this chapter, but for now it is important to know that they are significant. This doesn't mean that you must cuddle up with them, but at least recognize that they have some qualities that can help you solve major problems and issues in life.

When you are able to identify an important animal, what does it feed upon and / or what feeds upon it?

Most animals fall midway in the food chain. They feed upon and are fed upon. Looking at this animal and its relation to others will help you further with what is going on in your life. For example, let's say that you have skunk showing up in your life. Most animals in the wild usually only have one encounter with a skunk. Rarely is it deadly, but it is most memorable. They teach us to set boundaries that people will remember. If skunk is showing up, then you should also study the great horned owl because skunk is the favorite food of this great bird.

The great horned owl is one of the most powerful and aggressive birds of prey in this country. If you have skunks showing up, take a look around you. Who in your life has the owl characteristics? You will want to keep clear boundaries with that person. On the other hand it could also indicate that you need to become much more aggressive in setting your boundaries. In either case, you need to work with both the skunk and the great horned owl. Together they provide balanced medicine or power.

Unusual Ways of Identifying Totems

Over the years I have taught about a thousand workshops on animals and totems. In the early years of teaching it I would go around the room and give the major totem of individuals in attendance and explain quite accurately how that animal applied to the individual's life. I used one of the following methods to do this. All are effective, but they require a good degree of study, practice and development. Once accomplished though you have a tool for dealing with and handling other people in your life more effectively.

The auras of individuals reflect the animal.

Sometimes the aura of the individual will take the form of an animal whose presence is strong in the life of the individual. It takes practice to see the aura and since the average individual has an aura that extends 8-10 feet out in all directions, it can sometimes be difficult to discern the form. The animal will also sometimes appear as a shadow form in the aura, close to the person's body.

The posture of individuals reflect the animal.

How often have you heard people say something like, "he flits around like a bird" or "she moves like a cat"? Humans have often been accurately compared to animals by their behavior and movements. When you begin to study animals, you will notice specific postures, behaviors and movements that are inherent to them or their species. Some animals bob their heads. Some birds perch stoically, with feet spread and balanced. Some animals nervously shift. Some stand sideways to you. Some creep when they walk and some primp and put on displays. Many humans have similar postures and movements to the animal spirits that are strong around them. Paying attention to the body language of the individual and relating it to a corresponding animal with a similar body language is a very effective means of identifying animal(s) whose energy is core to the individual.

Psychic perception of the totem

A third way of determining a person's animal spirit is through the intuition or psychic perception, including communication from a spirit guide. When you look at another person, what animal comes to mind? What animal do you imagine he or she to be? This also takes practice, and it should be tested more closely than the other two. At least have some physical substantiation (the actual form of the aura and the actual physical movements of the person). With the psychic method, it is easy to project the animal you wish rather than what is. Feedback from the individual will help you to confirm and further develop your psychic skills so that in time this can be a trusted tool.

Skill
Development

Still Hunting

Benefits:

- **Develops serenity**
- **Increased ability to spot and observe wildlife**
- **Increased perception and understanding of Nature**
- **Enhanced intuitive connections to the natural world**

It is important to connect with Nature in a different way. Sometimes we shield ourselves so much that we lose the ability to experience fully. Sometimes we develop such a hectic lifestyle that we forget how to observe the subtleties of life. This is an exercise that can expand our perceptions and awareness of Nature and all of its inhabitants – plant, animal and mineral. It develops our intuitive connections to all of the natural world.

Begin by just meditating in Nature. Send thoughts and prayers to Mother Nature, asking for signs and communications. Choose different environments for your meditations. Quiet the mind in your backyard or a nearby park and pay attention to what you feel, smell, hear and see. Feel yourself become one with Nature. Try and feel the heartbeat of Nature resonating through you and your own heart beating in rhythm with it.

Once you have been meditating out in Nature, then it is time to take the next step – *still hunting*. Still hunting was practiced in shaman traditions all over the world. Its primary purpose is to observe and learn. The still hunter would go to a place in Nature he or she knew well or felt attracted to. There the individual settles into a quiet, watchful mood. If the arrival disturbs the wildlife around, the individual waits patiently until everything returns to normal. If you remain still, the animals in that area will return to their normal activity within ten minutes. Then the still hunter truly opens himself or herself to learn from the natural world.

If we wish to become still hunters, we must let the place choose us. Allow your intuition to guide you to a place in order to learn a lesson.

You must trust your mood, and once the place is selected, you must become as unobtrusive to the environment as possible. Still-hunting can be practiced anywhere, even in your own back yard. All that it requires is that you remain still and observe.

1. Plan on going by yourself. Taking someone with you is difficult because there is always the temptation to talk or even whisper, which will disturb the environment around you. If you do try it with someone along, make sure it is someone who knows the importance of quietness.

2. Let the world go on around you as if you weren't there. If you disturbed the environment upon your arrival, be patient. It may take some time (about ten minutes) before things settle, but it will as long as you remain settled and quiet.

3. Feel and imagine yourself as part of the environment – a part of the natural surroundings. Imagine yourself as the leaf rustling in the breeze. Feel the ticklish joy of the butterfly as it dances from flower to flower. Let the songs of the birds fill your heart, noting how it affects the body and where.

4. Quietly observe the various sounds, smells, movements around you. Note how the insects and animals respond to each other. If you must move and adjust your position for comfort, keep your movements slow and as infrequent as possible. The more still you are, the more likely you are to experience curious animals coming in for a closer look at you.

5. Pay attention to how animals and plants use camouflage. Note how they move. Begin to keep a mental log of the number and kinds of insects, plants and animals that you experience. Even if you can't identify them at the time, when your still-hunting is over for the day, you can use books and other tools to help you identify them.

6. Keep a logbook of your still hunting experiences. Keep track of dates and animals observed, and other unusual experiences. Write down your moods – what you felt as you had your experiences. Research fascinating facts about the creatures and plants you experienced.

As you practice your still-hunting you will find yourself increasingly observant. You will find yourself recognizing by intuition the presence of creatures before they become visible to you. You will find yourself observing more around you than you ever imagined. Remember that the greatest shamans are first and foremost great still hunters.

Skill
Development

Recognizing Tracks and Signs

Benefits:

- **Develops observation skills**
- **Increased perception of the presence of animals**
- **Enhanced intuitive connections to the natural world and subtle messages**

As we spend more time in Nature, we will begin to notice things that eluded our perceptions before. Most animals in the wild are good at camouflage, but even if we don't actually see the animal, we can confirm the animal's presence through signs. The most common signs are tracks, scat, food remains and digs. With any of these signs it is important to remember that if you noticed it, it is significant.

Tracks are prints, usually of the feet, left in the ground by the animal as it passed through the area. Track identification takes a lot of practice, but it is fun activity. Identifying tracks, noting size, characteristics and even making drawings of them is like being an amateur detective. Tracks alert you to an animal's presence and part of the fun is that you never know ahead of time whose tracks you may discover.

Four surfaces are best for registering the tracks of animals: snow, mud, sand and dust. Snow is considered the best, especially for following the animal over greater distances. Stops along the way provide information on its behaviors and activities as it travels. Mud makes good impressions, and you should look for tracks around the edge of ponds, creeks, dirt roads and puddles. Dust is not as effective, for recording long lasting impressions. Tracks in it are temporary. On the other hand, it will record the tiniest and softest of impressions, even the trails of insects. Sand allows you to follow a trail for a longer distance, but the tracks are rarely recorded in detail. Sand shifts and drifts a lot. Early morning and after rains, while the ground is damp, are good times to look for tracks in sandy environments.

When trying to identify a track, the following steps will help:

1. Sketch a drawing of it. This will help you later when trying to research it.
2. Make note of its size. Measure it. If you don't have a tool for this, use your fingers to help you estimate its size. You can convert your "finger measurements" to regular ruler measurements later.
3. Note the number of toes. This will help you eliminate animals and narrow down possibilities. The illustrations on the following pages will help you begin this process.

Scat is the waste droppings of the animal. The size and shape of the scat can tell us which animal might be crossing our path or in the immediate area. Some scats are distinctive in size, shape and even color. The average person more readily recognizes rabbit and deer pellet type droppings. Bird droppings are also usually recognized by everyone, but trees with a whitewash of bird waste, usually indicates a larger bird (crows, ravens, hawks, owls, etc.) that returns to this tree frequently, probably to eat. Hawks and owls will regurgitate the undigested parts of their prey (fur and bones) in the form of a pellet. . Checking around the base of the tree for pellets can be an aid in narrowing down the source of the whitewash.

Scat identification though is not an exact science, but its appearance when out in Nature is a solid indication of the presence of an animal. Some mammal scat is hard to distinguish. For example, fox, coyote and bobcat have very similar scat, so similar that it is difficult to tell one from the other. In that case other criteria must be taken into consideration. Which of these are in this area naturally? Are there any tracks to help pin it down.

For several months, scat was found on the driveway to my barn. We suspected it was coyote at first, but we had no other clues, other than it had to be a nocturnal mammal. It was always found in the early morning. Then it was found a couple times in the morning when skunk spray from the night before was still lingering. We began to study more closely about skunk droppings, and eventually, the skunk was seen. We had our confirmation.

Food remains / caches are signs of animals feeding on various kinds of matter. They alert us to the presence of certain animals. Middens are small piles of refuse. They are usually made up of nutshells, pinecones, and other matter when an animal eats at the same spot regularly. They usually indicate the presence of squirrels, chipmunks and mice. Mushrooms with small bites out of them can indicate the presence of a red squirrel, vole and even the gray squirrel. Branches piled in the water can indicate the presence of a beaver, but they are often found near the lodge. Skunks, raccoons and bears will often tear open hornets nest to eat the larvae inside, especially late summer and early fall. A study of animals indigenous to the area where the remains are found will help you to identify the particular species.

Digs are holes in the ground that animals use for homes and for pathways. Digs are some of the most common indicators of animal activity and presence around you. Anyone who spends even a little time in Nature will wonder who or what made a hole that they have found. This is not always easy to answer. (For the record though, snakes do not dig their own holes. They have nothing to dig with, but they have no problem using the holes that others have made.)

Voles, mice, moles and shrews dig holes and tunnels less than two inches in diameter. Red squirrels dig holes about 3 inches in diameter, but it is most often in an area of coniferous trees. This is because the cones are a major staple of their diet. Woodchucks dig major burrows away from the water and they usually have several exit tunnels. Their holes can be 6-8 inches across and a large mound of dirt in front often identifies their burrow. The opening is usually cleared of any leaves, sticks or anything that could block the opening. Fresh scrapings and a clean opening is usually an indication that the burrow is currently being used. Larger holes can be fox or coyote, and muskrats will dig holes into the sides of ponds and creeks.

Depressions are also a sign of animal presence. Deer will make larger depression in tall grass to sleep and rest. Rabbits use a small oval shaped depression called a form as a resting-place, next to a natural feature of the environment that offers protection.

How Many Toes?

(Most people can recognize a hoofed animal, but it is the track with toes that will give people difficulty. The following is a good guideline to begin learning how to identify common tracks.)

__Two Toes__

Deer and Moose tracks make two toes and are very similar. The moose tracks (3-7 inches) are much larger than a deer track (1-3 inches)

Deer / Moose Track

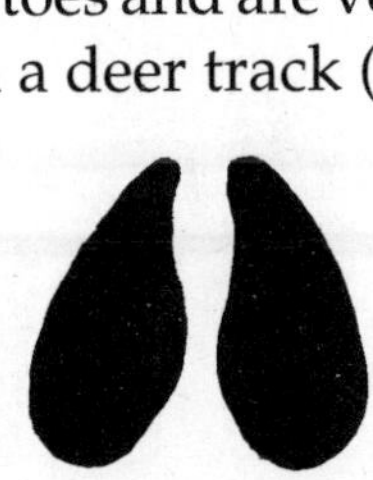

Four Toes

A number of animals have four toes: rabbits, cat, dog, fox, coyote, and bobcat. The dog, fox and coyote will have four toes with claws showing and are very similar. The fox track is a bit more oval in its overall shape though. Rabbits tracks are oval, rarely with any claws. The cat and bobcat are rounded and similar. The bobcat has a paw print 2-3 times larger than a house cat.

Rabbit Track

Fox Track

Cat and Bobcat Tracks

Five Toes

Members of the weasel family have five toes. These include weasels, minks, skunks, fishers, otters and badgers. Weasel tracks are tiny with the five toes having claw in front. Otter tracks reveal five pointed toes. Skunk tracks have five toes with claw marks in front of them, approximately 1½ inches long and 1 inch wide. Raccoons have tracks that look like miniature human hands. The opossum is similar to the raccoon, except the fifth toe on the hind foot is to the side and back, like a thumb. The muskrat track is also similar to the raccoon, except the inner toe is very small and barely shows in the track

Skunk Track

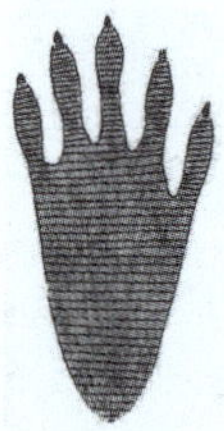

Raccoon

Opossum

Muskrat

Four Toes in Front & Five Toes in Back

Some smaller mammals have four toes in front and five toes on the back feet. Tracks like these can mouse, shrew, vole, red squirrels and gray squirrels. If tiny they are probably mouse or vole (less than a half inch).

Gray Squirrel
Front and Back Tracks

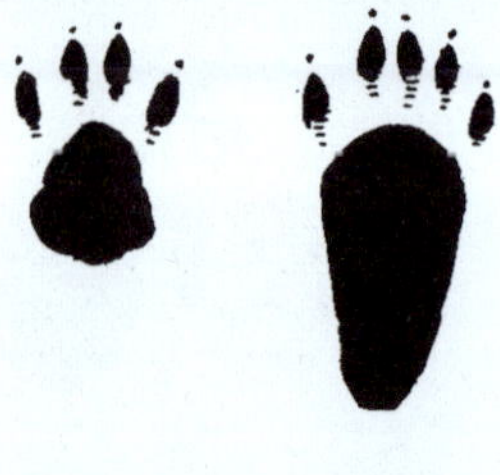

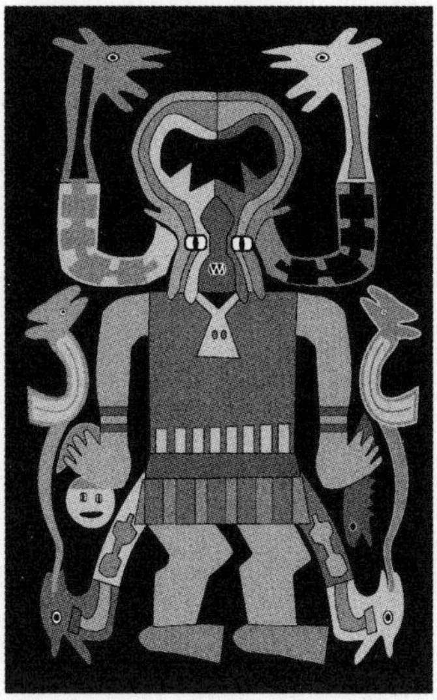

Skill
Development

Fear Totems

Benefits:

- **Develops ability to face fears**
- **Helps conquer long-standing issues & recurring problems**
- **Increases self awareness and introspection**
- **Helps identify important totems**

Have you ever found yourself asking, "Why does this always happen to me?" or "Every time I get so far something happens and it all falls apart"? Are there certain issues that you seem to encounter regularly throughout your life? Do you seem to run into the similar kinds of problems, conflicts and difficulties frequently? The answer to overcoming these problems, ending the patterns and accomplishing your goals more successfully may lie with the animal(s) you fear.

Animals that we fear are often our most powerful totems. Many traditions taught that our fears and doubts will take the form of an animal and only when we come to terms with those fears and doubts does that animal become a powerful ally for us. When we learn to incorporate the animal's qualities and medicine into our life, we are on our way to being able to walk through life without casting a shadow.

Animals we fear usually possess the characteristics and the power to resolve our recurring issues. This doesn't mean we have to learn to cuddle up with the animal, but we have to begin to recognize that animals we fear reflect major lessons in life. For example, if you have a fear of snakes, you may have come to learn how to handle transitions more effectively, to shed the old and move into the new in some important areas of your life.

The problem is that many of our fears are social fears. Society and people in society teach us to fear and be uncomfortable around certain animals. Two of the most common animals feared are snakes and spiders and yet both are amazing animals.

Snakes and Spiders, Oh My!

The **snake** is an amazing animal. From the moment it's born to the moment it dies, it never stops growing – a lesson most people can benefit from. It sheds its skin because it has outgrown it. When I was associated with Brukner Nature Center, I loved presenting snake programs. It provided a wonderful opportunity to breakdown misconceptions that many people have about this animal.

One of these is that the animal is slimy. It has scales, making them shiny, and many species will soak themselves in water before shedding. The water helps loosen the skin, but this makes them wet, not slimy. The snake programs were held in a room with a tile floor, and as with most tile floors, if there is foot traffic, it will accumulate dirt. I would ask the kids to wipe their hands back and forth across the tile floors around them and then hold their hands up to show how much dirt was on them. (Parents and teachers, of course, loved me for this.) Then I would take the tail of the snake and wipe it across the tiles as well. I would then swipe the tail with a white cloth, and there would be next to nothing on it.

First of all, this proved that humans truly are slimier than snakes. Second of all, it helped demonstrate that if there were any moisture attached to the snake, it would get bogged down as it moved through the grass and the dirt.

At the end of the program the kids were allowed to pet the snake. Inevitably, as I came around with the snake in hand and held it out to some adult, he or she would hold their hands up and say nervously, "Oh no, this is the kid's time." And everything I just tried to accomplish would be shattered. It sent the message that this still was something to be afraid of. Many of our fears are societal fears. They are passed on to us and not learned through any actual experience.

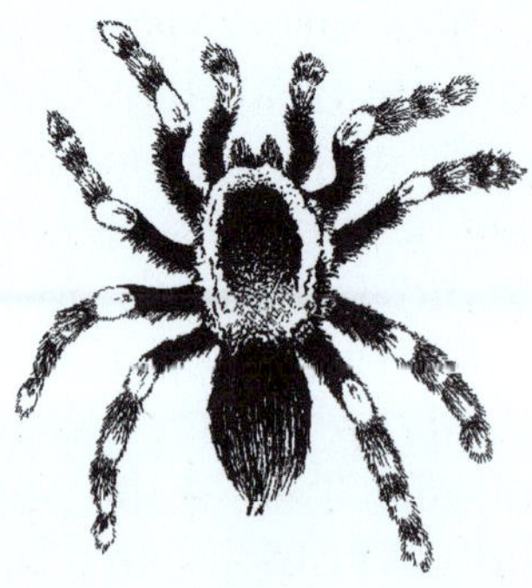

Probably the second most feared animal is the **spider**. Spiders are amazing creatures. They almost all spin silk, even though they all don't weave webs. Spider silk is believed to be the strongest natural substance on the planet. Most spiders that we encounter in the Northern Hemisphere are web spinners.

Do you know why spiders do not get caught in their own web? It is partly because they have an oil on their legs, but mostly it is because only some of the threads of the web are not sticky at all. The threads that go around the circumference of the web have the sticky. Those that go directly out like spokes do not have the sticky and this is what the spider uses. Knowing this then, if you come across a spider web when seeking answers from Nature, you have a very clear answer. Don't take the round about way of dealing with the issue at hand or you'll become entangled. Be straight and direct. If you have a fear of spiders, you may need to learn to be more direct in dealing with others.

Spiders have eight eyes, but they don't see very well. They have fibers on their legs that are sensitive to the subtlest movements. If you have spiders showing up in your life, don't trust what you see. Trust what you feel.

And for those of you who may have trouble sleeping at night, here's a little spider trivia that will help. They serve a very vital function in Nature. The insect population is the largest group of animal life on the planet. Spiders help to control that population. In order to do so though, they too must be quite numerous. In fact, they are so numerous that it is estimated that we are never more than three feet from a spider…

Pleasant Dreams…

So how do we handle animals we fear?

When there is an animal that you fear, it is *very* significant. It is one of your major totems. Knowing this does not mean that you have to learn to cuddle up with it, but recognizing it as such and learning as much about it will help you tremendously within your life. It is an animal that has qualities and characteristics that will help you accomplish some of your greatest goals and resolve some of your most difficult and recurring problems. The following steps will help you with this.

1. Study the animal.

Knowledge always conquers fear. The more we know about the animal, the less we will fear it. Go to the library. Go to the children's section of the library. Get a children's book on the animal. Most children's books will provide the most outstanding information and characteristics of the animal in a nonthreatening way.

2. Spend time around the animal.

Many zoos and nature centers provide opportunities to observe more closely and even touch various animals under safe conditions. Just observing the live animal through glass can be helpful. If it makes you squeamish, observe it for increasing amounts of time over several months.

It doesn't always have to be all at once. The more we are around something, the less strange it becomes to us. Familiarity breaks down prejudices and uneasiness.

3. **Examine major issues in your life.**
   Over several months time, take a look and write down major issues, recurring troubles, complications that are not unique. Most people have said or thought, "Why does this happen to me?" Well, what is it that always happens to you?

4. **Apply the animal's characteristics to your issues.**
   So now you have figured out some of the issues that always seem to resurface within your life. In the past, how did you react to them? Did you handle them the same way? Take a look at the animal's characteristics, how can they be applied to those issues and problems? For example, let's say that you have a fear of spiders, and you have trouble asserting yourself at work. Whenever difficulty arises, you hint at what the trouble is, working around it, hoping those who need to know will figure it out. If this hasn't worked before, it is not likely to work now. Do what the spider does. Be direct. Take the straight line and not go round about with your boss. The worse that can happen is it won't work, but the round about way hasn't worked either. You will be surprised at how applying the qualities of the animal you fear to the recurring issue will resolve it for you.

5. **You do not have to cuddle up with this animal.**
   Just because this animal is "creepy" and it is not furry or cuddly, does not mean that it can't benefit you. It has unique qualities and abilities, and these same qualities and abilities can be used by you to accomplish your greatest goals and resolve your most difficult problems. In learning to work with that animal you fear, you empower yourself and you acknowledge your own ability to heal, resolve, create and accomplish more than you may have ever imagined.

"What is man without the beasts? If all of the beasts were gone, men would die from a great loneliness of spirit, for whatever happens to the beasts also happens to man. All things are connected. Whatever befalls the earth befalls the children of the earth."

- Chief Seattle

Barracuda

I was at an intersection in my life. I was doubting my decision to leave teaching to pursue a career in writing. I had one of the best years teaching ever and it was hinted that if I stayed around for another year, I would be put in for tenure. I sought out several psychics and they all told me to stay with the teaching for another couple years, but it just didn't feel right. Everyone had a different opinion and most felt it was wrong to give up the security of a solid job at that time. Needless to say I was confused by all of the differing opinions. Finally, my wife said that I should do what is in my heart to do and that she would support whatever I chose. I turned in my resignation.

While scuba diving in Eleuthra in the Bahamas not long after doing this, I had some unusual encounters with a barracuda.. Every time I entered the water, whether diving or swimming, the same barracuda demonstrated aggression toward me. I began to get a little paranoid about being in the water. I could not get in without this barracuda coming after me. Our dive guide followed me around with a spear gun, poking at the barracuda whenever he got close to me.

It wasn't until late in this diving trip that I realized (through the reminding of my wife) that it was probably my necklace that was attracting the barracuda to me. Barracuda hunt by sight and they will attack any flashing metallic object. I understood that part and taking it off helped, but he still hung around whenever I was in the water.

I knew there had to be another reason and I began to do some research. Barracuda travel in schools when they are young, but as they get older, they become more solitary. They are often reminders that it is time to break away from the group. It is time to go off on our own - to follow our own path. Part of its message for me was to follow my own solitary path. And because they attack flashing objects, it was a reminder to do what I needed to do for myself but without a lot of fanfare, without the second guessing and without all of the opinions of others. It was time to quietly follow my own path.

Chapter 2

Understanding The Message

There was a time in which humanity saw itself as part of Nature and Nature as part of it. Dreaming and waking were inseparable. Animal and human were inseparable. The natural and the supernatural merged and blended. Shamans used the symbols and images of animals and Nature to express this unity and to instill a transpersonal kind of experience.

Because of our innate connection to Nature, animals still play a particularly strong role in our unconscious symbology. They reflect the emotional life of humanity, often reflecting qualities of our own nature that must be overcome, controlled and repressed as a toll of power. Animals are symbols of the archetypal power that we can learn to draw upon when pure reason no longer serves. This is why in most traditions around the world adopting the guise of animals and wearing their skins and feathers or wearing their masks symbolized endowing the individual with the animal's primordial wisdom and instinct.

Animal totems help us to see ourselves as part of the universe and they can be any kind of animal, for they each have their own unique medicine and power.

Terrestrial animals are often symbols of fertility and creativity that must be re-manifested in our evolutionary process. Each species has its own characteristics and powers to remind us of the archetypal powers we must learn to manifest more consciously. They are bridges between the natural and the supernatural. They awaken us to the realities of both. Terrestrial animals are warm-blooded and they teach us how to express love in various areas of our life. They teach us of our responsibilities in this incarnation and how to accomplish things in the physical world. They help us remain grounded, even while we explore the spiritual and less substantial aspects

Seven Rules to More Magical Encounters

1. Practice seeing and questioning as a child does. Be fascinated and filled with wonder about everything in Nature.

2. Be a naturalist first. Magic and spirit flows out from this and without the naturalist part, the magical shaman cannot be.

3. Take trips into Nature, at least once per season. Each season brings its own unique offerings and each season has its own lessons for us.

4. Find one special place for you to sit and observe regularly, a place that you can visit throughout the year.

5. Learn to observe and be curious about everything. Notice what is going on around you. Make notes or sketches of what you observe – plant or animal.

6. Be unobtrusive when out in Nature. Learn to be silent. Try not to talk. Just observe, contemplate and note activity. Don't smoke when out in Nature. It disturbs the environment and alerts animals to your presence. If you disturb an area upon your arrival, remain calm and quiet and within ten minutes it will return to normal.

7. Make your home environment attractive to wildlife. Hang feeders. Put up birdbaths and fountains. Have a variety of plants. Animal encounters occur in all environments, backyards and deep woods, urban and rural areas, waking and sleeping.

of life. They keep us connected to the tangible aspects of life. They help us to recognize and express our power while upon the Earth.

Terrestrial animals do not truly migrate. They are more nomadic. Because of this, they teach us how to seek out sustenance by simply altering our patterns and expanding where we put our efforts. They are also unique among other animals in that most terrestrials have a highly developed sense of smell. This is related to discrimination and discernment, a key role of terrestrial totems and messengers.

Birds in myths and tales are often symbols of the soul. Their ability to fly reflects our ability to rise to new awareness. They reflect the ability to link the physical realms with those of the sky (heavens). Birds link the waking with the dreaming. We are all given to flights of fancy, a phrase often used to describe our dreams and imaginations.

As totems and spirit animals, each bird has its own peculiar characteristics, but they all can be aids for inspiration, hope and new ideas. They show us the best way to move into new realms and how to follow our dreams. They have great eyesight and can help us to be more instinctively perceptive. They can open us to more psychic and spiritual perceptions. They teach the power of breath and the mysteries of air. They have always been considered some of the most important messengers from the spirit world, and those with bird totems will find that the realm of spirit will become more open to them.

Aquatic life serves as a dynamic totem. They link us to the reality of the dream life – sleeping or waking. Water is a symbol of the astral plane experience, much of which reflects it in our dreams. Water totems return us to our origins. There are many myths of life springing from primordial waters. Water is the creative element, reflecting the feminine archetype of the Mother. It is the feminine, the intuitive, and the creative that is brought to life when we dream or imagine. The moon, a symbol of the feminine, controls the tides upon the earth, and aquatic life teach us about the tides at play in our own life on many levels. They help us to move with the flow.

Fish and other forms of aquatic life make dynamic totems. They are some of the most adaptable creatures upon the planet, and when they appear in our life as messengers they can show us the best way of adapting to the environment around us – even those that might confound others. They have heightened senses, and fish totems always reflect a heightening of our psychic senses.

Insects and arachnids are also a powerful part of nature. The creepy crawlies make powerful totems and spirit animals. Most have ancient mythological histories. Most people look upon them as pests, but they serve a powerful purpose in the chain of life. They each have unique qualities, reflecting archetypal influences with which we can align.

All insects and most arachnids go through some kind of metamorphosis. At the very least, their appearance always tells us something about changes going on within us or around us. They help us to make the changes we may need in our own life. These animals are the natural shapeshifters, changing to ensure successful growth, and when any one of them shows up in our life, it is to help us in some way make the changes necessary for our own successful growth. This changing keeps their creativity alive and is a reminder that we must do so as well to keep our own creative energies strong.

Reptiles and amphibians are some of the most ancient creatures on this planet. They are cold-blooded creature, affected by whatever the temperature of the environment might be. Their appearance will always tells us something about our sensitivity to the world around us and about our ability to adapt to various environments.

Amphibians live in two worlds – part of their life on land and part in water. They reflect our ability to blend worlds and realms – physical and spiritual, male and female, waking and sleeping, etc. They can help us bring opposites together and bridge different realms of our life successfully.

Reptiles and amphibians hold the lessons about life, death and rebirth. They teach transformation and healing of some kind. The appearance of reptiles and amphibians can indicate the awakening of empathy – a heightened ability to feel the energies of others. They teach us to honor what we feel and to trust in it, because you will be more right than not.

Fantastic Creatures can also be totems. Although often thought of as part of the Faerie Realm, they reflect powerful forces in Nature. Some of the more common totems are the dragon, the unicorn, the phoenix and the griffin. Fantastic creatures connect us to some of the most archetypal forces of Nature.

The dragon controls the climate and thus teaches us how to control the climate of our lives. The unicorn is the most gentle and healing archetype found in Nature. Many healers have a unicorn as one of their healing totems. The phoenix teaches us the magic of life, death and rebirth, while the griffin holds the magic of protection of all things in Nature. Fantastic creatures remind us that magic is all around us. They remind us of our own magic and they often tell us that it is time to express it more fully.

Nightly Encounters

Animals that come out at night are called nocturnal. They have a special layer of cells behind their retina that reflects light, giving the eyes more chance to use what little light there is. This layer is called tapetum lucidum, and it is why nocturnal animals see so well in the dark.

The reflection that we see from headlights or flashlights is called "eyeshine". Different animals have different colored eyeshine, so even if we don't actually see the animal, we can help identify the animal through its eyeshine color.

Here are some examples of eyeshine colors:

Bullfrog - **green**

Night Heron - **red**

Opossum - **orange**

Owl - **yellow**

Raccoon - **bright yellow**

Red fox - **bright white**

Skunk - **amber**

How do I know if

"OK, let's say I step outside and I see a bird. Does this have meaning?"

Yes, it does have meaning. All animal encounters have meaning and significance. Not all of them are direct messages to us about something in our life, but they do have meaning. Sometimes the meaning is just environmental. It is a reminder of the beauty surrounding you. It is telling us to take time to smell the roses. Pay attention to the wonders. Listen to the haunting songs. See the beautiful colors and smell the sweet air.

"But I see that bird every day when I step outside, so it is just part of the environment. What meaning could that have for me?"

There are two kinds of animal encounters: ordinary and the extraordinary. Seeing a bird as you step out the front door may be an ordinary encounter, just a general reminder of the wonders of Nature. But seeing that bird fly right in front of you and land on your car may be a bit more extraordinary. Unusual behaviors and encounters make it extraordinary and alert you to a more personal message.

Many times our encounters are ordinary environmental encounters. The animals are just a part of our natural environment. This does not mean they aren't significant. Sometimes they are reminders to pay attention to the wonders around us. They keep a sense of wonder alive within us. Do not lessen their importance though. Animals that live in the same environment that we do are doing so successfully. Thus, they can teach us how to live more successfully within that same environment.

"I live in the city. I'm not going to have some of the encounters others talk of. How am I going to connect with my totem or get an animal messenger?"

There are many ways of encountering animals, even in the modern world where most people live in urban environments. A great many animal species exist in urban environments. Modern cities are homes to mice, rats, squirrels, opossums, raccoons, foxes and coyotes. In both urban and suburban areas bears and even mountain lions occasionally appear. Birds of every variety are found, from the tiny chickadee to hawks, vultures, owls and eagles. And we have a multitude of insects, spiders and reptiles. I lived in the city 20 of the last 25 years and I had some of my most amazing encounters in my own small back yard and neighborhood. Animals are around us, no matter where we live, , but encounters do not have to be face-to-face. This is a common misconception. You do not have to physically cross paths with the animal to get a message from it. The encounter can occur in other ways.

the animal is a message bringer?

"So what are some of the other ways we can encounter animal messengers?"

If we dream of an animal it is the same as meeting it face-to-face in the waking. It should be treated just as significantly. Maybe every time we turn on the TV there is a program on a particular animal. We open a magazine and there are photos of it. We see images of it on billboards, posters and it seems as if we see it every where we turn. We can have a variety of encounters, and when we have several of them within a close time frame, we should pay attention. The animal's's archetype and energy is manifesting in our life.

Let's say, for example, that every night while driving home from work this past week you drove through clouds of skunk spray. This is an encounter. You get home and you turn on the *DISCOVERY* channel and there is a program on skunks. You flip the channel to the cartoon network, and there is "Pepe LePew". You walk into a store and there are stuffed skunk toys jumping out at you. These are all encounters. And in this case, it's a lot better way to encounter the skunk than face-to-face.

"How do we tell the difference between animals encountered because they are part of our own living environment and those who may actually be our spirit animals and totems and have a more specific import to us at the time? Or are they one and the same thing?"

Experience is the key, and sometimes it is just developing that "inner knowing". There are though two tangible signals that can help us. *First, look for unusual and out-of –the-ordinary behaviors.* I am around a lot of animals every day – a wide variety of wildlife. Because of this, I sometimes need the animal to stand out in a more unique way through its appearance and/or behavior so that I know it is significant. For example, seeing an owl is very rare. They are nocturnal and they are very well camouflaged. Hearing an owl is a much more common experience. To see an owl then is a real good indicator that it has a message for you. If you see an owl in the daytime, you are getting what I call a "clue-by-four" up the side of your head. You're getting thumped with the importance of the encounter.

Secondly, if the animal is a message bringer we will have a variety of encounters with it, all within a relatively short time frame. If the animal is of significance for us, it will make its presence known to us in different ways and on more than one occasion. If we dream of the animal and then see it on TV, in stores and in other ways all within a few days, then this animal has a message for us.

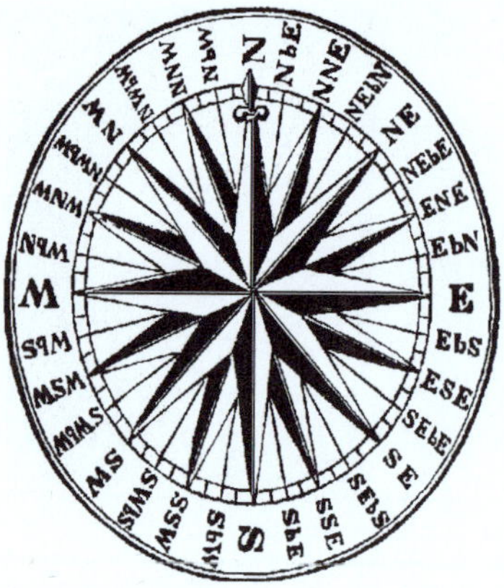

Understanding the Message

The ancient shamans were scientists, as well as mystics. They studied Nature and animals. They sought out answers and directions by studying, observing and applying what they learned to their daily lives. They knew that only by studying Nature and animals could the gifts of the natural world truly become ours, could they get the direction they needed for their lives. The difficulty though is in determining the significance of our encounters. Is the animal just part of our normal environment? Or does it have a more direct message for us? And if it does, how do we interpret the meaning of animals within our lives? This is not always easy to determine.

Learning the language and significance of our animal encounters is not always easy. This book and its predecessors will help, but the answers are not always readily apparent. Learning any language can be time consuming, and when it comes to a symbolic language we must guard against superstition.

Sometimes it will be obvious what the animal means. That skunk, which has shown up, may not have to do with boundaries at all. It may simply mean it's time to take a bath. Start with the obvious and then move on to the more intricate interpretation.

At other times it will require some effort to determine the meaning of the animal. Most animals that show up will apply to our life on more than a superficial level. They are frequently multidimensional, reflecting things going on in our life on several levels. By studying the animal and its qualities in relation to people and issues in our life, we begin the process of determining its significance Begin by asking four significant questions and then proceed to the more in-depth exploration of the meaning:

- When we have the encounter with the animal, examine what we were focused upon at that time. What were we doing and/or thinking about at that time? What was most on our mind?
- What have we been most focused upon in the couple hours prior to the encounter? In the previous 24 hours?
- What major issue(s) have been occurring within our life?
- Are there new things we are starting? Have we already or are we about to take up some new endeavors or activities?

In-Depth Guide to Interpretation

When we have significant encounters, it is because that animal has something to teach us. It has shown up in our life to show us how to accomplish a task, resolve a problem or remind us of what we are capable. Learning to interpret the message effectively will save us a lot of frustration in our endeavors. We increase our chances of success tremendously.

Study the species of the animal encountered.

All species of animals of the same type have qualities in common. All reptiles share qualities in common, as do mammals, birds, insects, arachnids, and amphibians. These qualities speak generally to you about something going on in your life or something you should be doing.

Determine if the animal is predator or prey,

Most animals in the wild are both predators and prey. Some are distinctly one or the other. Some are more aggressive, some more passive. Some stand their ground when threatened and some move to avoid threats. How does the animal you have encountered handle threats, surprises and the presence of other animals around it? Determining whether the animal is a predator or prey will help you to determine how assertive and aggressive you should or should not be in handling situations going on around you.

Examine the specific animal.

Every animal has unique qualities and characteristics that set it apart from the rest of its species. This animal has appeared in your life because it has qualities specifically beneficial for you and for what is going on in your life. Some animals rely on eyesight, some on hearing. Some animals develop natural strength and power, while others develop stalking skills. Some animals put on displays and develop unique coloration to attract, distract, romance and alarm. This animal's appearance is a reminder that you have these same potential abilities and characteristics and using them will help you at this time. For example, a hawk that misses capturing a rabbit does not pretend it's a weasel and chase it on foot. It must learn to fly faster, strike harder and hold tighter. It is true to its unique abilities. If hawk has shown up in your life, success is much more likely if you spot, strike and grasp the opportunities when they present themselves.

Determine its biological rhythm.

Every animal has its own unique life rhythm, times when it is more active, aggressive, procreative, etc. It has a rhythm that enables it to survive more successfully. Some animals hibernate and some are active year round. Some are active at night and some are active during the day. This animal has appeared to tell you that its rhythm is at play within your life.

When we place our own individual schedule into that of the animal (as best we can) we align ourselves with a more universal rhythm at play in our life. For example, young bears will stay with the mother for up to two years before going out on their own. If bears have appeared in your life, a two year cycle may be coming to an end or you may expect your efforts to take two years to truly mature and come to fruition. Although determining the rhythm involves some trial and error, when you hit the right rhythm things begin to click around you. Activities and energies flow and fall into place.. There will be less strain and force required in finishing, resolving and accomplishing things in your life.

Study the adaptive behaviors.

Every animal adapts to survive. This includes the use of camouflage, remaining still, playing dead, and never following the same path twice and other behaviors. This animal has shown up in your life to tell you that its adaptive behaviors will work best for you right now. Use them.

Crows, for example, will gather and mob birds of prey that come into their territory. They are particularly aggressive with owls. They instinctively know that if they do not drive the owl away, it will come back at night when they can't defend themselves and have one or two of them for dinner. This mobbing is an adaptive behavior. If you have crows showing up in your life and you have problems, don't try and handle them yourself. Do what the crow does, get some help and gang up on the problem.

Examine what is happening in your life.

Look for issues, problems, new activities that you are involved in at the time of the encounter. Are you undertaking new tasks, making changes or moves, trying to solve conflicts and problems? Make a list.

Apply the animal's qualities to what is happening in your life.

Learning to apply the animal's characteristics and energies to your life and yourself takes practice. It involves analysis, reflection, intuition, some trial and error and even some testing as to whether it truly applies. One of the best ways of doing this is to do some kind of analysis. It doesn't have to be as intricate as the example on the following page. It can be simply a list of the animal's characteristics along side of a list of issues, activities and endeavors currently on-going within your life. It can also be a bit more formalized, as part of your own personal animal messenger field guide, as described in the exercise at the end of this chapter.

So What about that "Wascally Wabbit"?

Let's say, for example, that rabbits are showing up in our life. The rabbit is an animal with a very mixed symbology. Among the Algonquin it was kind of a demigod. In Egypt it was a hieroglyph that represented the soul or being. To the ancient Hebrew it was considered unclean, because it was so prolific. It did what rabbits do best – procreate. To the ancient Chinese and Japanese there was not a man in the moon but rather a hare in the moon.

When we study the rabbit, we find that of all of these interpretations, it is the Asian that is the closest. Young rabbits are capable of being out on their own at 28 days. Twenty-eight days is the lunar cycle. When rabbits appear in our life, there is a cycle or rhythm of 28 days (or one month) at play. This is their ***biological rhythm*** and they have shown up to tell you that this is the rhythm at play in your life.

All animals adapt to survive in the wild, and the rabbit is no exception. Rabbits, mice and rats are the most common prey animals. Most predators recognize prey by movement. The rabbit has the ability to freeze in order to avoid predation. This is an ***adaptive behavior*** not a fear response. A hawk sitting in a tree does not think to himself, "I had rabbit last night. I think I'll wait for a nice squirrel to come along." The hawk recognizes potential food by movement. A rabbit's ability to freeze is a way of not being eaten.

Because they are one of the most common prey animals, they relate to their environment by being very prolific. They will have several litters in a year to ensure their survival as a species. This is an ***adaptive behavior*** also. If rabbits are showing up in your life, be involved in as many creative projects as possible within your environment. Some may not make it, but some will!

And rabbits do not do things in a step-by-step fashion. They move in little hops and jumps. They have a wonderful ability to backtrack and make up lost ground. These are some of their ***unique abilities***. So if you have to backtrack, you will be able to do it in jumps and leaps, making up lost ground quickly.

I love it when rabbits show up in my life. It is always an indication that I will not have to invest a great deal of time and energy into something before I see results. If something is occurring in my life when rabbits appear and I am not sure what to do, I freeze. I do nothing. It doesn't take more than 28 days before I know exactly what I must do. And even if I have to backtrack, I will make up lost ground.

The Meaning of Colors in Nature

Nature is filled with colors and the animal kingdom has some of the most unique varieties. Colors camouflage, warn, attract and repel, but all colors in the animal world have meaning for us and should be explored when we have encounters.

Black - One of the most common colors of animals found among all animal kingdoms; associated with mysticism, magic and new birth; a color of quiet strength and protection; may be a need for secretiveness and sacrifice.

Blue - From blue birds to a variety of moths, this is a color reflecting truth and happiness; energy of expressiveness and increased perception; be careful about loneliness or faultfinding; time for more social interactions.

Brown - One of the most common colors of Nature and animals, it is always a reminder to stay grounded; often denotes a time of practicality and strength; can also reflect a tendency to be overly critical at this time.

Green - Found among insects, reptiles, sea life and birds, this is the color of Nature; usually reflects something about growth, abundance and healing in our life; need to move through emotional imbalances and uncertainties.

Gray - Found among all animal kingdoms, this is a color of ancient teachings and clarity of mind; reflects a need to trust in the imagination or a need to keep it in balance; color of clouds and fog, it can reflect things are hidden from us at this time.

Orange - Color of warmth, it is most often found among the insect, bird and reptile kingdoms; reflects new energy, new creativity and new joy is at hand; balance your worries and recoup your energies.

Red - In nature this is a color that is striking, wherever it is found; it is a color of sexuality, passion, strength and it is attention-getting – often warning others away or drawing them near; be careful about impulsive and aggressive behaviors.

White - Found in all animal kingdoms, it reflects the energies of truth and spirits are about us. Albinism occurs in many species and usually reflects a strong spiritual message; be careful about scattering energies.

Yellow / Gold - Common among the bird and insect kingdom, this color usually reflects issues of communication at hand; trust in your inspirations and avoid being overly critical.

The Meaning of Numbers in Nature

Birds gather in flocks. Some mammals live in herds. Some animals pair up for life. Some form family groups. Some animals are social. While others remain solitary. The number of animals that you encounter can be significant and help you determine further meaning. For example, crows usually appear to me in threes. This is often an indication for me that the magic of creativity and new birth is calling to me. Whether it's the number of the animal seen at one time or the number of times the animal is encountered within a week, it is helpful to explore the meaning of the number.

One - time to initiate; new beginnings; take charge - leadership role may be upon you; be careful about coming on too strong or domineering.

Two - time for a partnership or dealing with a companion; has the energies of the dreams; issues of intuition and cooperation at hand; be careful about meddling.

Three - time of magic and new birth; creative imagination is very active and should be worked with; express yourself but be careful of gossip.

Four - time for a new foundation and for patience in laying it; issues of groundedness and stability are at hand; focus on the practical and avoid being too stubborn.

Five - time of change and movement; lots of activity is at hand and will require versatility; make your moves but do not become scattered.

Six - time to focus upon yourself, your home and your family; energies and issues of feeling safe within your personal environment are at hand; control your worries and be practical.

Seven - time to seek out and explore the spiritual and mystical energies at play in your life; trust in the wisdom of your animal guardian; issues of trust surface; be careful of where you put your faith.

Eight - time of power is at hand; issues of money (a symbol of power in our society) are prominent; be careful about being careless or greedy; trust in your own power to do.

Nine - time of healing and completion; issues of endings and new beginning surface; energies of transition and leaving the past behind; be careful about being overly sensitive.

Poisonous and Dead Animals

"What does it mean if the animal is poisonous?"

Many animals in the wild are venomous and toxic. Most of these are found in the insect and reptile kingdoms. Almost all spiders have toxicity in their bite. Most would be no more troublesome than a mosquito bite or a bee sting, unless there is an allergic reaction. When there is an encounter with an animal that has some toxicity to it, there are usually issues at hand about the chemistry of your life. Your own body chemistry may be changing. This may be due to healing that is necessary or through natural changes that occur periodically within our life. Adolescence and menopause are two common times when venomous or toxic animals show up as messengers and guides.

Sometimes the meaning of these encounters is more symbolic. It may reflect that the chemistry of our life is changing. It may be telling us something about the changes to our relationships with family and friends or about jobs and activities that are no longer beneficial to us.

"I keep seeing road kill. Are the animal's qualities are dying in me?"

Unfortunately, we live in a time and a place where the natural world intersects with the human world. And sometimes there are causalities resulting from these intersections. It does not mean that the animal's qualities are dying within you. I operate under the premise that all things are significant, and if we notice an animal alongside the road, it has a message for us. It's amazing how many drivers do not notice animals hit on the road. The fact that you did makes it significant. Examine what was on your mind at the time you noticed the animal. Sometimes, the noticing is not so much a message for us, but to us to help the spirit of the animal move on. Say a quiet prayer for the spirit of the animal. It honors the animal and helps keep sacred your bond as a Steward of the Earth.

"Animals come into my backyard and die. What could that possibly mean?"

Although it is sad when such things occur, it is a special honoring of you. Injured and sick animals are very good at camouflaging weaknesses. Most sick and injured animals show no signs at all of their condition until it is too late. In the wild any display of weakness, opens them to predation, so they camouflage or they try to find a safe place to heal or die more peacefully.

They have found in your environment that safe place – a sanctuary. Animals instinctively know where to go to feel safe. They have honored you by coming to you. Acknowledge it, honor their passing and remember that they have blessed you by coming to you at their most vulnerable time.

Skill Development

My Nature Journal

Benefits:

- **Increases understanding of animals**
- **Improves observation skills**
- **Crystallizes spirit energy behind encounters**

When we begin keeping a record of encounters in Nature and follow it up with some study, we become naturalists. The Nature Journal is a log of your encounters. It is a personal field guide for you to observe and note activity and ultimately apply its meaning to your life. It is a record of your animal messengers. It can be used for dream encounters as well as all waking encounters.

This journal or field guide is an important aspect of moving to a deeper level of understanding the spirit behind your encounters. It is what helps us develop the mindset that *everything has significance*. More importantly, when you record your experiences, they truly become yours. Each experience becomes a drop of wonder in your life and this makes your own well of magic deeper.

When we explore the significance and energy associated with our experiences then we are becoming more than just a naturalist. We are becoming animists or spiritists. Animism in anthropology is the belief that all of Nature has spirit and these spirits are closely connected to humans. Animists recognize and believe that everything in the phenomenal world is alive and has spirit. These spirits are often intelligent and have the ability to communicate and interact with humans.

Spirituality is not determined or limited by knowledge, reason or creative intelligence. Our teachers are not merely the human ones. Our learning and guidance can come from sources other than human. Divine messages are not limited to coming to us only through those of "our kind".

When we realize this, our world is no longer the same. Your Nature journal helps crystallize this for you.

The journal activity should be used for all significant animal encounters and all journeys into Nature. It should have two parts. The first is to note what you observe and it should have space for follow-up research information and conclusions (possible meanings of the encounter).

Although some people use separate notebooks for both, I recommend using just one. Simple is always better. A good spiral notebook is simple to use and easy to carry. Then adapt the following sample page guide to suit your own needs. In time, you will adjust it anyway, finding the way of noting and recording that is best for you. You will surprise yourself how much more you will notice and remember when you record your encounters.

Sample Nature Journal / Field Guide Set-Up

Date:

Location:

Animals observed & their activity:

(Use border areas for sketches)

Follow-up

Research:

1. What is this animal's normal life cycle or rhythm?
2. How does this animal adapt to survive?
3. What are the unusual skills and abilities of this animal?
4. What is its normal environment and how does it relate to other animals in it?
5. Is this animal a predator or prey animal?

Determining the meaning:

1. What was most on your mind before the encounter?
2. What has been the biggest focus in the past few days?
3. What major emotions or issues have you been focused on?
4. Are you considering starting anything new? Ending something? Making changes? If so, what qualities or characteristics of this animal might help you accomplish this more easily and effectively?

Skill
Development

Getting Simple Answers

Benefits:

- **Develops recognition of Nature communications**
- **Develops the intuition**
- **Improves knowledge and relationship with animals**

Shamanism teaches us that *all* forms of life can teach us. By studying and reading about animals, birds, fish, insects, reptiles, amphibians and more, we learn about the qualities they reflect in our self and our life. This is essential to understand when we discover our true, personal spirit animals and totems. The more we learn of our totems, the more we honor the archetypal energies that affect us through them- the more we honor the divine potential within ourselves.

Nature is talking to us all of the time. Because of this, we can go to Nature to get simple and quick answers to problems and questions in our life. It begins with asking for answers or insight and then taking walks in Nature to get those answers and insight.

1. Ask for communications whenever you start something new.
One of the best things about my travels are the opportunities to see animals on the longer trips, and whenever I teach a new subject for the first time, I especially look to see what animal shows up on that trip. About 10 years ago, I was teaching my first workshop on making spirit animal masks and how to use them in healing and meditation.

The workshop was about an hour and a half from where I lived. On the trip to the workshop I did not see a single animal. I did not see a bird, a mammal or an insect. I did not even see the hawks that always watch out for me when I travel. This was most strange, and needless to say I was more than a bit concerned. I was pretty sure that the world was about to end.

When I arrived at the workshop in the early evening. Everything was set. There was a group of about 40 people. We made beautiful masks. We did a wonderful healing meditation with them, and by the time I left, I was very confused. As I pulled away, and started down the road, my headlights caught the eyeshine of an animal. I slowed down, assuming it was a dog or cat. As I reached the corner, there was a raccoon sitting up on the sewer grate watching me as I drove by.

Now I was completely lost. I was more than halfway home when I had one of my sometimes-frequent forehead slapping experiences. Raccoon! Masks! Duh! Raccoons have a natural mask. Their paws are also quite agile and capable of subtle manipulations. Well we were using our "paws" to make masks. They are also nocturnal, and so it was not appropriate for me to see them before I arrived at the workshop. Now every time I teach that workshop, raccoons are there at some point. Raccoon is a totem that guides the energy of that seminar.

When you start something new, take a few minutes to meditate or pray, asking for guidance from some aspect of nature to watch over the activity. Ask that it make itself known so that you can honor it. When we start to ask, we get our answers.

2. Take answer walks in Nature.

In a process similar to the first, if you have a problem, take a walk to find out your answer. Remember, nature is talking to us all of the time. Most of the time, we miss the communications. If we have a problem or need some guidance, sit and meditate upon it, praying for nature to provide us with a message.

Then take a walk in the woods or in a park. Even take a walk in your neighborhood. Do not talk to others. Reflect on your problem or situation. Make sure the walk lasts about a half an hour.

At the end of the walk what aspect of nature stood out or kept coming up. Was a particular fragrance? Maybe you smelled pines. Pine fragrance is calming to emotions and feelings of guilt. It may be telling you that you are getting too emotional about the problem. A study of the plant or tree will provide some clues as to its meaning.

Was there a particular bird or animal that caught your attention? Maybe there was a blue jay calling off and on. Blue jays often indicate assertiveness and reflect proper and improper uses of power. It might indicate a need to take advantage of the opportunity or to assert yourself more.

Do not worry that you might be imagining it all. The particular aspect of nature would not be catching your attention or coming to mind if it did not have significance for you.

Be specific in your questions. The more specific you get as to what you should do the better and more specific the answer will be. Ask what behavior you should demonstrate in a situation. Then observe what behaviors you most see in the animals on your walk. When you start applying these answers and when you then study the animal, you will gain even more insight and you will start to recognize more and more subtle communications.

Avalon

I have shared my life with many animals over the years. In fact currently more than 20 animals are part of our home. My wife and I have shared our residence with cats, dogs, rats, guinea pigs, horses, a scarlet macaw, a jandaya conure and several hawks. (Although, the hawks really are not pets.) All of them have things to teach us, and their behaviors when they stand out are usually reminders of something we should be doing as well. Their behaviors are messages to us, especially when we take notice of them.

Kodi was the alpha dog, but she was always the lady. The other dogs would often try to cut her off when let into the house to eat and drink. She just trusted her position in the pack and remained calm. Whenever I noticed this, I would take a step back and look at what I have been thinking. Was I trusting in my position and status? Her behavior was often a message to be patient and wait; my position was not threatened at all. If my dog Cheyenne, who was usually standoffish and a loner, became friendly and pestered me to play, it indicated that I needed to take some time off, socialize and play a little.

Avalon was almost 16 when she died this year. She had several small strokes and was even run over by a power company truck when they came to read our meters on the farm. Her hips were bad and barely supported her and she dragged her foot when she walked. But with all of this she carried on as if nothing was truly wrong… well, unless she didn't get her food at the scheduled time. She was as playful as one her age could be, smiling throughout the day and still enjoying walking to the barn every morning. She followed me around when I mowed the lawn and she even took the occasional walk with me through the woods. She was a daily reminder that we must do what we have to do and no matter what life hands us, we can still find enjoyment in the day. She was truly a treasure and a wonderful teacher.

Chapter 3

The Power of Domestic Animals

All animals, wild and domestic, have their own unique abilities. They have varying degrees of intelligence. They have a great ability to show love, fear, anger and other emotions. They have spirits that are strong and although some might disagree, they also have souls.

Animals have served a great but often forgotten purpose in our development. We are exposed from the time we are little to myths and tales, books, cartoons and movies involving animals that speak, love, play and even solve problems. When most of us learned our alphabet, it was with the help of animals. "A is for ape, B is for Bat, C is for cat, D is for dog…" We have experienced through media influences what shamans and medicine people have taught for thousands of years. Animals do speak. They deliver messages and they call us to greater awareness.

I am frequently asked in interviews why I believe that my books on animals do so well. I believe that it is partly because everyone has a story about animals. Almost everyone has had some unusual or moving experience involving animals, if only from their dreams. Animals fascinate people – whether wild or domestic. Animals touch people, often without people realizing. Animals provide a spiritual tie to the Earth. I believe there is an unconscious recognition that animals reflect archetypal forces within the world, reminding us of the primal sources from which we came.

Part of the shamanic tradition is connecting to the primal and universal energies of the Earth and to *all* life upon it. Pets and domestic animals are often the first step to this reconnection. Today's world is often one of sensory overload and our pets and other domestic animals provide a link for us to those universal energies without feeling further overwhelmed and overloaded.

What Our Pets Can Teach Us

1. Past Life Connections

Animals return, as humans do, to learn and to grow. Often they will incarnate with humans that they have been closely connected to in the past. Sometimes an animal that has served as a totem may return as a pet. Where the pet originated also often reflects locales of our important past lives, the lessons of which are playing out currently in the present.

2. Behaviors we need to express

When we notice a behavior of one of our pets it is something to pay attention to. They will often demonstrate behaviors that reflect our own or are ones we need to express more fully. When mine pressure me to play, it is often an indication I am working too much.

3. Skills in accomplishing tasks

Pets have their own unique qualities and characteristics. They have skills that they can teach us. Cats know about everything that goes on in their environment and can teach us how to notice things as well. They remind us of skills we need to incorporate as a regular part of our life.

4. How to bond and love more unconditionally.

Animals love unconditionally. Regardless of the day they have had, they greet us, run to meet us, meow and bark at us. Even if we are out of the home for an hour, when we return we are greeted as if it has been days.

5. How to communicate with animals more clearly.

As we learn to communicate with our pets, we are learning how to communicate with other animals as well. We learn to use and to read body language. We learn to project thoughts and exchange thoughts with our pets. We begin to read the subtleties, emotions and projections of our pets. This can be applied to wildlife, which we will explore later in this book.

6. How to recognize the presence of spirit

Pets and animals of all kinds are often much more sensitive to the presence of spirit. They recognize subtle energies at play within their environment. Paying attention to them will help us to be more alert to the presence of spirit.

Most traditions did not teach that domestic animals were true power animals. They recognized that domestic animals could have significance and they were often used in metaphors of a positive nature. The true totem though was the wild counterpart of the domestic animal. The domestic animal was what the individual worked with until he or she was able to handle the more primal energies of its wild counterpart.

For example, the dog would not be the true totem. Instead you would look to the wild member of the canine family – the wolf, coyote, fox, jackal, dingo, African wild dog, etc. For the cat, you would look to the wild member of the feline family – bobcats, tigers, leopards, lions, etc. The nice thing about cats is that you can often look at the cat and figure out what wild member it looks like. "Oh, that cat looks just like a little tiger" or "He looks just like a panther".

This is not to say that we don't learn from our pets and domestic animals. There is much to learn from everything that we experience in life, and shamanism teaches us that all forms of life can teach us. This is especially true of the animals closest to us. When we realize this, then even domestic animals, particularly livestock, will no longer represent the worst qualities of people in society. Every animal – wild and domestic - has its own unique qualities and personalities. And when we honor our pets and domestic animals, we are also honoring the primal essence behind them.

In order to make the transition from domestic to wild, we need to examine how we treat both differently – aside from our ability to encounter them. Then we must begin to relate to them in a more similar and effective manner. We name our pets. They become personal to us. We speak to them, holding sometimes-lengthy conversations. They are often sounding boards. We tell them of our day, our troubles, our hopes. And most pet owners would probably agree that their pets understand them or at least their tone.

Most people though do not speak to the wild animals in this way. It is almost an assumption that because they have so little contact with us that they could not ever understand us. But if we learn to talk and relate to wild life as we do our domestic animals and pets, we may be surprised at the response. Wild animals will no longer become mere spectacles but spiritual creatures of great power and complexity.

This is not to say that by being able to relate to your pets and domestic animals that the wild kingdoms will open up automatically to you. Nor does it mean that by giving wild animals a name, we will open to their power and they will become petlike. What will happen is that we will begin to notice the communications that come to us daily from the less domestic side of nature. We will begin to understand wild animal encounters more fully. When we understand our pet's behaviors and apply that to understanding wild animal behaviors, we will see similarities. And this returns us to our instinctive ties to the rhythms and lives of the natural world.

Your Pet as a

Animals are gifted with heightened senses. Homing pigeons always find their way back home. Horses sense electrical changes through their feet and are thus able to avoid lightning strikes when out in a field. Dogs and cats sense whether there is fear in humans around them.

Most people know that I work with birds of prey. Because I use them in educational programs, they have to be socialized to be around humans. They are not pets and so this is not a natural thing for them. One of the ways, in which I have done this in the past, is by bringing them indoors while I go about my daily activities. This gets them used to human movement and activity and thus they are not as likely to be nervous in front of groups.

I am always amazed at how sensitive they are. I have found that the wilder the animal is, the more instinctually and psychically sensitive it is. My hawks are always the first to pick up the presence of spirit in my home. Their heads will turn in unison in the direction of spirit.

Then it's my cats. Cats have not been domesticated nearly as long as dogs have and so are still fairly quick at sensing the presence of spirit.

My dogs, on the other hand, are kind of "doh…dee…doh…dee…doh…" They are always just a bit slow in picking it up…bless their hearts.

All pets detect spirit much quicker than we do. Their instincts are more defined and practiced for sensing subtle changes in their environments. By paying attention to changes in their behavior and how they respond we can become more aware of spirit around the home as well.

Spirit Detector

How to know if your pet is detecting the presence of spirit:

1. Staring intensely at an area in which nothing is there.
This will not just be an idle daze on the pet's part. It will be a deliberate and focused stare at a specific spot. Often they seem to be looking directly over our shoulder.

2. Running through the house, chasing and barking at things not present.
Our home is also our pet's home and all animals try to protect their territory instinctually. They guard it against intruders.

3. Growling, snarling and hissing at what isn't apparently there.

4. Avoidance of entering a room that is not usually avoided.
This can sometimes be accompanied by whining and submissive postures.

5. Staring at doorway, windows and corners of the rooms.
All intersections are places where there is a thinning of the veils between the physical and the spiritual. Most people who see spirit often do so in doorways, windows and corners. These "Tween Places" are natural intersections. A doorway is neither in nor out; it is in between.

When we encounter these behaviors or any that seem to indicate the presence of something unusual by your pet, take a moment to sense for yourself. It doesn't mean that your home is now haunted or that you are being visited by evil spectres. Relax. Take a few deep breaths. Close your eyes. What do you see? Do you feel anything different? Is there a particular person that comes to mind? (Often loved ones return to make their presence known, to let us know that they are still with us.)

Mysterious Behaviors of Cats & Dogs

Many behaviors of cats and dogs often seem mysterious. There are some very probable explanations for them.

Cats

Kneading

Cats knead to seek comfort. As kittens they knead their mother to stimulate her milk. They may knead on a warm human or a woolly blanket for comfort just as they did as kittens.

Rubbing forehead and cheeks against you

Cats have scent glands underneath the skin, and this is the cat's way of marking you with his scent. He is claiming and acknowledging you as his own.

Playing in paper bags

Cats use paper bags, boxes and closets as safe hiding places where they can peer out and practice checking out situations before they begin their hunt.

Dogs

Jumping up to lick the face

This is not an aggressive behavior. It is a re-enactment of puppy behavior with its mother. It is a submissive behavior. It is a greeting of us as higher ranked member in the pack. It is a way of seeking comfort from the owners.

Howling

Howling serves many purposes. It sometimes reveals the dog's location to other members of the pack. Some dogs howl for loneliness, celebration and even alarm. For some dogs it is their way of singing.

Anal Sniffing

Dogs have an anal-sac-gland secretion that can contain as many as 12 distinct scents. It transmits a wealth of information, such as sexual status. It is used to mark territory and for other purposes not completely understood.

Domestic Animal Dictionary

Cats

Keynote: magic, mystery, and skilled pursuit

All cats, domestic and wild, have a great deal of myth and lore about them. Although domesticated, the cat retains much of the independence and power of its wild counterparts. Wild and domestic members of the cat family have much in common and are often attributed contradictory meanings – devil and angel, guardian and attacker, good luck and bad luck. It is an animal associated with curiosity, independence and even healing.

The cat was sacred to the goddess Bast in Egypt and was associated with the goddess Freyja in Scandinavia. It is even associated with the goddess of childbirth in India. It is found in myth and lore throughout the world.

Most cats are nocturnal and the nighttime has often been associated with magic and fear and things mysterious. Cats alert us to things not readily visible to us. Cats have more rods in the retinas of their eyes, which allows them to see very well at night. They perceive what we may not. And they are excellent at detecting the presence of spirit. Cats can see in near dark – giving them a decided advantage over most prey at dawn and dusk. Their eyes are rounder, giving them a wider view. This vision is but one trait that makes it a great hunter.

Cats also have the ability to smell 5-10 times more accurately than humans do. One of the main functions of this sense of smell is to detect the presence of other cats. This sensitivity is partly why cats have often been associated with guardianship, especially against things magical. This also helps them to stalk. One of the lessons that all cats teach is how to go about stalking or capturing in a quiet, stealthy manner.

A cat's ears are very sensitive, hearing a wider range of sounds than humans. Its ability to pick up high-pitched sounds is how it is able to detect the presence of a squeaking mouse. The outer ear can also swivel that allows them to pinpoint sounds more accurately. Cats teach us to listen more closely to what is not readily being said.

The pads on the cat's feet are soft, allowing him to sneak around without anyone hearing him. Because the cat's claws are retractable, there is no clicking sound. (In the wild, only the cheetah's claws are not retractable.) The cat teaches us to be quiet about our pursuits. That is what brings the swiftest and greatest success.

The cat is an animal that has developed many skills and qualities necessary for a truly successful hunter. When any cat appears, it has the ability to teach you how to pursue and capture goals, answers, and anything else in your life more successfully.

Most cats appear to be a smaller version of a wild member of the feline community. This is often the best way of determining which member of the wild feline family is the true totem. For example, some cats look like little tigers, some like panthers, some like bobcats and so on. Your cat, aside from having its own unique powers and energy, will help serve as a mediator or bridge to the wild counterpart.

Today there are many breeds of cats, each with some unique coloring and characteristics. A closer study will help you to determine the unique lessons and potentials that your cat brings into your life. Many books exist on the lore of cats, and so further study is always warranted. Regardless of the breed of cat, when one appears in your life as a companion and messenger, new magic, mysteries and skills at pursuing your goals successfully.

Chicken and Rooster

Keynote: new birth, fertility and sexuality

One of the first birds domesticated, the chicken has developed a tremendous amount of symbolism. It is a descendent of the pheasant and because of its egg laying ability, it is often associated with fertility and new birth. Gods and goddesses were often invoked to bless a home while performing the simple act of throwing grains to feed the chickens. Its egg is an ancient and powerful symbol for new birth and new life. The presence of chickens usually indicates on some level opportunities for new birth, new endeavors and fresh beginning.

The rooster is the male of the chicken family and is often associated with sexuality. It serves an entire brood of hens and fertilizes their eggs. It crows with the rising sun and so is also associated with the birth of a new day. In Chinese astrology, it is associated with energy and enthusiasm.

The appearance of a rooster or of a chicken usually heralds a time of new birth and renewed energy. They are symbols of optimism and new creativity. They herald the promise of fertility.

Conures

Keynote: deepening relationships; family and young require attention and careful expressions

Conures are part of the parakeet family. There are many varieties, and they are often kept as pets. Conures are known for their loud voices. (Their screeching is what makes them and most parrots difficult pets to have in apartment environments.) They also delight in destroying and chewing woods. For little birds they have powerful beaks. The old adage, "His bark is worse than his bite", does not apply.

In the wild they are found in tropical areas of Central and South America, and they are very colorful. A study of their qualities of color will provide some insight into their individual energies. Two of the more commonly known species are the Sun and Jandaya conures.

The male Sun conure only spends the night in the nest, and both parents feed the young. In eight weeks the young are completely independent, and even among most conures, the young become quite independent very quickly. This is often a reflection of their significance. Creative endeavors often mature and become independent quickly. It also often indicates a rhythm of 8 weeks at play within our life.

Another common conure is the Jandaya. Its head and nape is a bright yellow, and its underside is an orange red. The wings are mostly green, and like their relatives the Sun conure, they can be quite loud and vocal. Unlike the sun conure though, the males will spend the night and most of the day in the nest. Both parents feed the young. This is a reminder for those in relationships, family or business, to share in the care of the young – be they children or projects.

In nearly all species of parrots and parakeets, the beak is an amazing instrument. It can be employed almost like a third foot when climbing. Thus all parakeets show us how to accomplish tasks with what we have available. The beak is designed for removing husks and breaking up plant food. It reflects increased ability at discerning and "getting to the heart of matters" for those to whom the conure appears.

Between its loud screeching and its beak we gain some special insight to all species of this and other similar birds. The voice is our most creative instrument. We can use it to make a person feel as if they are standing in the shadows of the divine or wish they had never been born. Conures reflect this ability. They are reminders that our words will have an increasingly greater effect. Things written or spoken more gently will be experienced more gently. Things spoken or written more harshly will be more devastating. Learning to control how we express ourselves will become important.

Conure nests have great significance in the importance of a "true home". It is not used just during the breeding season but year round. In the wild, even the fledged young will return to it regularly to roost. What we say and how we say it will have a great impact upon our children and their independence. Others who will learn from us will use the foundation.

When conures show up we must be careful to choose our words and activities carefully. They will have a greater impact upon those who are closest to us. Are we being too critical or harsh? Do we need to take our responsibilities more seriously? Are others around us not fulfilling theirs?

Conures are wonderful signs of potentially deepening relationships and responsibilities. The bonding between most pairs is very deep, and there is often partner feeding outside of the breeding season. They reflect greater opportunities for balance – especially in the home life, but the home will require greater attention and more careful expressions of caring than before.

Cow and Bull

Keynote: fertility, motherhood, nourishment

The cow is a powerful symbol of fertility and motherhood. It is an animal that provides nourishment without being slaughtered. It is a lunar symbol and is especially sacred in the Hindu tradition. The cow is the giver of mother's milk, and thus it is a reminder of our need to draw upon the energies that the Earth provides naturally. Its appearance can indicate a time of nourishment and plenty or a need to seek out further nourishment.

While the cow symbolizes the lunar, the bull reflects the solar. It is the fertilizing force. It is strong and powerful and reflects the need to assert one's creative energies to stimulate new fertility and growth.

The bull is associated with the sign of Taurus, a sign associated with possessions and fertility in mundane activities. Cows and bulls promise that fertility is available to us while we walk the Earth. But they are also a reminder that for that fertility to create abundance, we must assert our efforts and be productive. They ask the question: "Are you being as productive as you can be?"

Dog

Keynote: companionship, fidelity, security, and understanding and use of body language

Humans have utilized the dog for more than 10,000 years. In spite of that there is relatively little folklore, especially when compared to the cat. In ancient Persia and China superstitions and folklore abound in relation to dogs. The Fu Dog in China is a recurring symbol bringing happiness and good fortune. The Egyptian god Anubis was jackal-headed and assisted souls in crossing to their final judgment. The role of dogs in folklore and literature opened up though in the last several hundred years.

Dogs are close relatives to wolves. Next to humans, the wolf is the most widespread of all social predators. It was found throughout Europe, Asia and North America. Dogs are distantly related to coyotes, jackals, foxes and other wild canines, such as the African wild dog. When we have a dog as a companion, it is a link to one of these wild members of the canine family.

The dog is known for its fidelity and its guardianship. It provides us with companionship and even healing energies. It is a pack animal and the pack works together to find a source of food, protect the food, and to protect the territory. Pack behavior is well defined. There is an alpha male and an alpha female, and rest of the pack follows the lead. Working as part of a group to succeed is part of what dogs teach us. They remind us to look at our role and how we fulfill it.

Although it has a variety of barks, it communicates most effectively through body language. It is intricate and effective. Every dog can teach us how to use our own body language more effectively in accomplishing tasks.

A dog's senses are similar but sharper than that of the human. Its eyes are more sensitive to light and movement. They detect slight movement easily, which alerts them to possible prey. Its ears allow it to scan the environment for sounds. It can detect sounds four times farther away than humans and it can locate the source of a sound in six hundredths of a second.

Touch is the first sense a dog develops and is important throughout its life. Its entire body is covered with touch sensitive nerve endings. It reminds us of our need to touch and be touched. It reminds us that we need intimate companionship.

Smell is the dog's most advanced sense. A large part of its brain is developed to interpreting scent. It has a scent-capturing organ at the roof of its mouth A dog's sense of smell is enhanced when it moves quickly, more air moves through the nose. This is helpful because dogs hunt by chasing down prey. They remind us that we must pursue or chase what we seek.

The dog's ability to perceive on so many levels makes it a wonderful guardian and social hunter. Because of this dog teaches us how to accomplish things more successfully by pooling efforts.

There are many breeds of dogs and each has its own unique qualities. Terriers have an aggressive instinct. They work ruthlessly without backing down when confronted by foxes or badgers. They willingly engage in head-on combat with earth dwelling mammals in their territory. They are often expert tunnelers, and they teach us to dig in and aggressively go after what we seek. Some dogs are workers, i.e. spitz-type dogs, Chows, Pomeranians and Malamutes. Humans have used them as valuable workers. They teach us how to be more valuable and productive in our own work efforts. Herding dogs guard the home, property and livestock. They look after livestock like their own pack. They help us in guarding and protecting what is ours. Hounds serve their own unique purposes. Hounds usually are sight or scent oriented. Sight hounds are bred for speed, teaching us to act quickly on opportunities. Scent hounds have great stamina in pursuits. Sporting dogs are used in the hunt and capture of prey and help us with this in our own lives. They teach us how to pursue, capture and flush out opportunities.

Examine the qualities of your breed. Even mixed breeds will have mixed and very useful qualities. Pay attention to your dog's behavior. If something stands out for you, note it and try to apply it to your life. A dog is a powerful animal with ancient links to primal energies. It reminds us and teaches us the importance of faithfulness, and companionship in our pursuits.

Guinea Pig

Keynote: sacred and social communing and healing

The native people of South America ate wild cavies or guinea pigs. Around 5000 BC the Incas domesticated them. They were used in religious ceremonies and as food. When the Spanish conquered the Incas, they brought some of the guinea pigs back to Europe, and it became a popular pet among aristocrats during the 1600's.

One theory as to how it got its name is because its meat tastes like pork. Another is that it looks like a miniature pig. Yet another is that the guinea is a mispronunciation of Guyana, a country where European traders acquired the animal.

The guinea pig is a cavy, a rodent related to the capybara. For those to whom the guinea pig has appeared as a totem or messenger, a study of the capybara would also be beneficial. The guinea pig, as with all rodents, can reproduce quickly. Females can bear young when they are only one month old. It lives in social groups called herds. Because they have no natural defense, they use the herd for protection. They create trails between burrows so they can always find cover when danger approaches.

The guinea pig is linked to great spiritual healing in South America. It is believed to have the power to remove illness, appease spirits and help people pass from one stage of life to another. Often animals that have burrow systems are animals whose spirit helps us bridge to new realms – whether of healing, safety, spiritual or more.

When the guinea pig has appeared as a totem or messenger, New realms will open up. People who think and believe more like you, no matter how different your beliefs will come forward. There will be more communing and participation in spiritual activities, sacred rites of passage and more.

If the guinea pig has appeared in your life, then it is time to explore some new possibilities. Are you ignoring your early spiritual and religious associations? Do you need to reintegrate them? Are you being too solitary in your spiritual practices? Do you need to seek out groups to help with your healing work? Are you ignoring the opportunities to involve yourself in healing activities?

Now is the time to initiate or reopen spiritual doors and passages of sacred communion. Those of like mind can join together for great healing work.

Hamster

Keynote: preparation, organization and curiosity

The hamster is a member of the rodent family, most common to Syria and other Middle Eastern countries. Its name comes from the German word "hamstern" meaning "to hoard". It refers to their cheek pouches in which they store and carry food back to their burrows.

There are many species of hamsters, inhabiting semi-desert areas. Some of the more common domesticated species are Russian, European, Romanian, Turkish, Tibetan and Mongolian. They live in burrows with many tunnels. They have separate chambers for food, sleep and other aspects of their life, thus their association with organizational skills. Hamsters can help us become more organized and prepared.

Some species have expandable cheek pouches in which they carry food and bedding to their burrows. They store food in great quantities, and they are usually a reminder that we should be prepared and keep our own stores up.

Hamsters have large incisor teeth that grow throughout their life. They must have something to chew on to prevent the teeth from overgrowing. They are also curious by nature, and those to whom the hamster is a messenger will find that they need something to sink their own teeth in. They are reminders to study and explore things, which arouse our curiosity.

Hamster people are usually loners, except when mating. Too much time with other usually leads to fighting. They do breed rapidly though and have the shortest gestation period of all mammals – 16 days. They live about two years, but they can have a new litter each month with ten or more young in the litter. This is an adaptive behavior that allows its species to survive. Hamster people often seem to move from one creative project to another, constant activity and change. Not all work out, but the numbers work to their benefit.

Horse

Keynote: new journeys, power, telepathy

The horse has had much symbolism throughout the ages. It has reflected the spirit, astral travel, and a guide to other worlds and dimensions. It has been associated with death and birth and it has touched the mythology and lore of every major tradition.

Horses fascinate most people. Sitting upon and riding one raises us above the ordinary. It renews our sense of power. Riding horses has been likened to flying by more than a few traditions upon the planet.

But the symbolism of the horse is complex. It represented movement and desires. For many people, horses allowed exploration and freedom from the constraints of small communities. It allowed them to travel greater distances.

To the Native Americans horses were companions, guides and great teachers. Observing their behaviors taught them much about plants, seasons and relating to one another. They also believe that horses communicate with each other and with humans. I believe that horses have a great ability for telepathy, picking up on the emotions and thoughts of those they are around, even humans.

At its core, the horse is a herd animal. It needs companionship and its appearance in our life tells us something about our own need for companionship and it can teach us how to relate to others in new and unique ways. They teach us how to take our proper role in our community.

The horse is also a prey animal and responds to threats and alarms like any prey animal. It also has developed unique senses to assist in its survival. They have lateral vision, which allows them to perceive wider range within their environment. They have an acute sense of smell and rely on it in all sorts of ways. They use it to identify members of the group and their home surroundings. They teach us to trust in what "smells right for us" and our own sense of smell is often heightened with the appearance of the horse in our lives.

Touch is also an essential component. It is used as a means of communication between horses and between horses and humans. Whiskers on the muzzle allow it to sense what it cannot see. Often people with horse totems develop good psychic touch perceptions themselves. Horses gain confidence by touching strange objects with their nose and the foot. Stimulating the sense of touch and smell. For those with horses as totems, it will be the touching of others that develops trust and confidence. Trust in what you feel more than what you see or hear.

A horse's hearing is much more sensitive than our own. The ears are easily rotated so that it can locate and focus and respond. Sight in horse though is a bit unusual. They often have a wide lateral vision but poorer frontal vision. This lateral vision allows them to lower their heads and graze and still be aware of their surroundings.

As mentioned above, I have come to believe that horses are very telepathic. They have great psychic ability. Many anecdotal reports exist of horse refusing to pass by haunted places. They also have an uncanny ability to sense danger and to detect the moods of their handlers and riders. They communicate through body language and read the body language of others around them with great accuracy. They can help teach us this.

There are a variety of horses – each with its own unique abilities, and the horse still serves a variety of functions. To understand your own particular horse totem, you must first determine its breed. It will help define the energy about you and even your purpose in life.

Draft horses (shires, Clydesdales, Percherons, etc.) are gentle giants. They have great power, stamina and a gentleness about them that makes them unique. Gaited horses (such as the Tennessee walker, the saddlebred, the trotter, etc.) have a unique gait that allows them to have a smooth ride and often reflect a more comfortable journey ahead. Quarter horses were named for their speed in the quarter mile and they can awaken power and speed within us. Arabians have flash, speed and charisma. Every breed has its own unique qualities and characteristics.

Examine the horse's color. Look at the characteristics it was bred for. All of its aspects are ones that it has come to awaken within you. Horses are creatures of beauty, grace, speed and intelligence. Horses bring with them, new journeys and adventures. They teach us how to ride into new directions. They take us to new discoveries about our own power and abilities.

Macaw
Keynote: sharp vision, spirit perception, sunshine and healing

There are a variety of macaws – scarlet, military, blue and gold, green winged. All of them are brilliantly colored, and although there is never just a single keynote for any bird, macaws are foremost birds of the sun.

Native to Mexico and Central America, archaeological evidence reveals that the Pueblo imported them and their feathers were as important in ritual and ceremony as the feathers of eagles and turkeys. Evidence seems to indicate that they had a preference for the bright red feathers of the military and scarlet varieties. The military macaw was honored for its ability to descend to the ground in May in parts of Mexico and eat poisonous ava nuts. They were a sign of new light that would swallow up the dark around an individual or group. It reflected the return of the healing sun.

The blue and gold is a larger species of macaw. Its color is most significant - as with any macaw or parrot. Its blue and yellow feathers are balance and were often associated with the directions of north (yellow) and west (blue). Its appearance often reflects the direction to look for healing and balance.

The scarlet macaw- as with all macaws - is a member of the parrot family, and it is found in rain forests areas of Mexico, Central America and South America. Its bright plumage made it a favorite among native peoples of North, South and Central America. Mythologically, all macaws are linked to curative and healing powers – especially of the sun.

They are intelligent, perceptive, brave and alert. Though they always appear calm, they rarely miss anything that goes on around them – as if everything around them is being exposed to new sunlight. Because of this the scarlet macaw's appearance indicates a tremendous increase in spiritual vision and perception.

In the Amazon, the scarlet macaw is linked to natives known as the Jaguar People, who believe they came from the stars. When it came time for them to return to the heavens, scarlet macaw was sent to gather them up. Some of the people were accidentally left behind, and when the gods discovered this, the scarlet macaw was banished to the Earth to serve as guardian and messenger for these people until the gods returned once more to take them home to the stars.

When the scarlet macaw appears our spiritual vision and perceptions are heightening. It will be sharper and more accurate. We should trust it, no matter how bizarre or strange the perception might seem. The macaw's appearance always heralds a time of greater spiritual depth and creativity. People will seek out our counsel, and we are likely to find new creative ways of expressing our perceptions and performing the counseling.

Scarlet macaws can live a long time, estimates are 75 to 90 years, and they are colorful birds. Their appearance always indicates the beginning of a long period of creativity and higher perceptions. Although they mimic human speech, they have an intricate body language and a variety of vocalizations that reflect a heightened ability to communicate more colorfully and effectively. People will pay attention and listen as never before. When the scarlet macaw appears, our vision, our creativity and our communications will brighten all that we do.

Macaws have powerful beaks, used to break open nuts. They show us how to crack open to gain the fruit of life. In the wild they often are found to eat a particular kind of clay, and they belief is that there are minerals within it essential to their health. For those to whom the macaw appears, there will be a need to watch and possibly increase the minerals within our own life.

Scarlet macaws are very emotional birds. It has been theorized that they have the emotional development of a 2-3 year old child. They respond to emotions around them in creative ways. If the macaw has appeared in our life, our own emotions may be coloring our vision and perceptions. We may perceive only what we want to.

The macaw often reminds us to look at health issues. If there are health problems, they may be emotionally related. We live in a time in which we know that emotions affect physiological processes. Balancing the emotions at this time will benefit physical imbalances as well. Learning to control the emotions is important now. The appearance of the scarlet macaw may also reflect a need for some sunshine and some color in our life. Color therapy can be of benefit. In the wild scarlet macaw also have been known to eat and dig in clay cliffs. The theory is that they derive some minerals essential to their well being from it. An examination of our own mineral intake may be important now.

If the scarlet macaw has shown up, we should ask ourselves some important questions. Are we seeing things correctly or through rose-colored glasses? Are we not being understood? Are our emotions unbalanced? Are our perceptions being used for gossip? For what purpose are we using our spiritual and psychic perceptions?

Parakeet
Keynote: messenger and companion

The parakeet or "budgie" is an Australian member of the parrot family. In the wild they are a grass green with a bright yellow head and long tapering blue tails They can mimic other sounds, including human speech, and thus they were often thought of as the messengers from other realms and distant places. They travel in flocks and are always with others of its kind. They are extremely social. Hence its other keynote – companionship.

When the parakeet appears one of two things is usually going on in our life. Either we are about to have some new companionship, or it is time to get away from the crowd and spend some time alone. The message is always though about whom we are or are not associating with.

The parakeet is a traditional messenger symbol not unlike the crow. In Egypt it was a symbol of the soul. The Persian poet Farrid Ud-Din Attar tells a tale of the parrot/parakeet that seeks out the waters of immortality and how it encounters various companions.

There are many species of parakeets, and each has its own unique qualities. But even with their uniqueness, they are always the messenger companions.

Pig (Including boars and wart hogs)
Keynote: fertility, fidelity, strength, and family protection

The pig and the boar have had sometimes an ambivalent meaning. If a sow crossed your path it was a sign of disappointments coming your way. If a sow crossed your path with a litter, it was a sign of good luck. The pig and boar were symbols of fidelity and strength, but also of intrepidness and irrational urges. It was sacred in Babylon. The savior god of India, Vishnu, once incarnated as a boar.

In the Celtic tradition it was associated with distinction and positive character. The Celtic moon goddess was sometimes depicted as the sow, the shining one. Many of the Celts venerated the boar as sacred to prophesy, protection and magical powers. Druids referred to themselves as boars because they dwelt in the woods as solitaries.

In other places it had other similar meanings. In Scandinavia, the god and goddess Frey and Freya both rode boars and provided protection for warriors. The maternal sow was often a symbol of the Earth goddess. The Tibetan adamantine sow is the Queen of Heaven, the Moon and Fertility. The female boar and pig were often fertility symbols because of its large litters. "Lucky pig charms" were made in Europe and America for fertility and prosperity, as well as lustiness in the home.

The wild boar is the forerunner of the domestic pig. Different societies had their own species of boar. Most of what people in the US experience is the European wild boar, but the Chinese and Indian wild boars are closely related to it. They are sometimes classified as the Eurasian wild boar.

Wild boars and their relatives are wonderfully adaptive to thick underbrush type of environments. Because of this they can show us how to maneuver quickly and powerfully through areas of congestion within our own life.

Boars range from gray to brown to black, and they have bristle, sparse hairs on the body which helps protect them against the thick brush in which they live. Because of this they are wonderful animals for helping us when we need some thicker skin - when facing the innuendoes, accusation or any negative words and projections of others.

The wild boar also has a disc-like snout that it uses for rooting. The boar can grow to 5 feet (150 cm) and can weigh up to 400 pounds (180 kg). The tusks may grow as much as 12 inches and are used for protection and for digging food. The boar and pig are excellent animals to help us sniff out and root out the treasures and delights. When the boar shows up, it is always a reminder to that if we want the treasures, we must dig them out for ourselves, relying on our own strengths.

Warthogs are part of the boar and pig family. It is found in mostly open fields in Africa south of the Sahara. It has a shovel shaped head with tusks. In males there are two lumps or warts on each side of the snout near the tusks.

Warthogs can inflict severe wounds with their tusks, just as boars can. For the most part tough, they are rather inoffensive, but they are powerfully protective of babies. The lion is its predominant predator, and so it should be studied as well.

Boars are surprisingly fast and powerfully strong. They usually live in small family groups in open woodland. The old males remain solitary.

They are unceasingly protective of the young. In European heraldry, the boar is powerful symbol of strength and family.

The boar or pig is one of the twelve signs of the Chinese zodiac. It is a sign associated with a cheerful and patient disposition. Boar people are encouraging to others and very honest, sometimes to the point of being naive. The boar person is generous and diligent in pursuits, especially in pursuit of the good life for their family. It is sometimes a symbol for sexuality. "Eating roast pork" is a Chinese metaphor for sexual intercourse.

When the boar appears, it is time to examine our fidelity and protection of the family. Are we us being unfaithful? Are those around us being unfaithful? Do we need to assert our family strengths? Do we need a show of fidelity, especially to our children? When members of the boar family appear, it is time to hold true to our standards of strength, faith and family. Are we not using our creative abilities? Do we need to look for more fertile life activities?

Rat

Keynote: industriousness, success, active

The rat is a very misunderstood animal. They are intelligent, clean and as pets they are very friendly. They are eager to please and eager to train. The domesticated rat comes from the brown rat and it is often referred to as the fancy rat.

Rats are members of the rodent family and their front teeth grow continually throughout their life. Thus they need things to chew on in order to prevent their teeth from becoming overgrown. For those with rat as a messenger it will be important to find activities that you can sink your teeth into and chew on.

Rats are also master architects. They are constantly rearranging their home environment, stacking, building, and adding on. Recently in England I was doing some promotional animal readings. I was discussing with a bookstore owner how the rat was an important messenger for her at that time. She coined the phrase "rat feng shui", which was quite appropriate. They are architects and will rearrange their homes until it is completely top their liking. They teach us the importance of this as well.

Their homes are usually organized and clean. They have places to sleep, places to store food and places to go to the bathroom. Their presence always is a reminder to stay neat and organized.

In Chinese astrology the rat holds the preeminent first position. It is an animal associated with success, industriousness and activity. People born in the year of the rat easily demonstrate these characteristics.

Rats are very prolific. In the wild if two rats have babies, and their babies have babies and so on, within one year there can be over a million rats. Rats remind us not to limit our activities or efforts. Involve yourself in as many creative projects as possible. They all won't make it, but a higher percentage will. Rats awaken our instinctual energies to survive and succeed.

Rats are also social animals. They live in packs and when rats show up within our life it is an indication that we need more social activities or that the present ones will increase tremendously. When rat enters your life, use your intelligence and shrewdness in all of your dealings. Trust your instincts and energies to handle multiple projects and activities.

Sheep

Keynote: sacrifice and abundance

The sheep was an animal often used in ritual activities. Moses initiated Passover through the sacrifice of a lamb. And it was often used in such ways in various religious traditions. The lamb has always come to be associated with purity of the spirit in its association with Christianity's Jesus.

It was a symbol of wealth. The number of sheep he had often determined a man's abundance. It had two main functions – providing food for nourishment and wool for clothing. These were two necessities for survival.

The fleece has tremendous significance. In the Greek tradition it was symbolic of great rewards, as in the heroic tale of Jason and his quest for the Golden Fleece. It could be woven into garments and cloths that provide warmth and covering for the body.

Sheep are usually watched over by dogs or by shepherds. These guardians protect the sheep from predators and other threats. When the sheep is part of our life, there is often a guardian coming into our life as well. It is an indication that with watchfulness, we can avoid difficulties and increase our abundance. It is not unusual though to get unexpected outside assistance at times.

Sheep in our life or as messengers remind us of the need to sacrifice the smaller for the greater. It is a reminder that there is abundance ahead for us. All we need be is watchful and trust in a higher process at play within our life, which may not always be visible to us.

Skill
Development

Past Life Exploration Through Pets

Benefits:

- **Awakens awareness of past lives**
- **Deepens connection with our pets**
- **Reveals life issues & lessons brought from the past**

When we look at the origins of our pets, we have clues to past life connections. Past lives and reincarnation mean different things to different people. Reincarnation is the return to the physical body. It is the belief that the soul upon death leaves the physical body and prepares to come back into physical life with another physical form. The circumstances of that return are determined by the growth and progress achieved in previous lives.

Beliefs differ as to whether animals reincarnate. Some traditions believe that they move from less intelligent forms of life to more intelligent forms of life. Some areas of the world have taught that the soul can come back as anything within the physical – from a tree to an insect to another human being. If you accept that animals also have souls – albeit not as developed as a human soul – then they would reincarnate as well.

We may never be able to prove that our pets or us have lived before, but that is not the purpose here. The purpose is to look at our animals in a uniquely different way. We have all met people that we felt we have known before. There is a comfort and familiarity about them. The same is true for our pets. Often there is one or two that seem extra special to us. There is a familiarity. It may have to do with past life connections.

Our present life is a culmination of many lives in many places, each with its own unique lessons and rewards. Some of the lives are still affecting us in the present. They may have lessons for us that we never quite completed or goals we never quite accomplished. Our pets and their origins provide clues to those lives still affecting us today.

We know, for example, that all dogs are descended from wolves. Wolves were found throughout the world. In different parts of the world though, the domesticated wolf was eventually bred and trained for unique functions and purposes. By exploring the origins of your dog, you have a clue to a past life locale whose energies are still affecting your present life. Your dog's behaviors and unique characteristics then reflect the lessons from that past lifetime that we need to polish and the skills and gifts we need to use more effectively.

In what part of the world did your pet originate? The Percheron horse originated in France. The Arabian originated in the Middle East. Domesticated hamsters originated in the Middle Eastern countries such as Syria. Cats have come from Egypt and a multitude of other countries. Dogs have come from all parts of the world. Where your pet originated often indicates an important past life influence in your present life.

1. Determine the origin of your pet's breed.
Most dogs and cats origins can be traced somewhat. Some cats developed in Egypt, some dogs in Russia. Horses and other domesticated animals have their unique origins as well. And even mixed breeds can be traced to some basic root.

2. Examine the countries that the pet's wild counterpart is found naturally.
For example, is your cat's wild counterpart a tiger? If so, then examine those countries where tigers are / were found naturally.

3. Explore some of the history of that country.
Every country has its own lessons and issues at play. In the United States a common theme is finding the balance between freedom and discipline. Often just by getting an overview of a country's history, we discover some similar lessons at play within our present life.

6. Look at the qualities of your pet.
Examine the unique behaviors and characteristics of your pet. What was this animal bred for? How was it used in the past? How can you apply those same qualities and characteristics to your present life?

Skill Development

Riding Through Time

Benefits:

- **Develops psychic vision**
- **Expands all perceptions**
- **Helps past life exploration**

Horses are amazing and magical creatures. They have great intelligence and great power. They have always stirred the imagination of humans and because of this they are powerful allies in taking sacred journeys.

Horses were critical to the spread of civilization. Without them, travel and expansion was limited. The horse allowed for new lands to open. This exercise employs the magic of the horse to opens us to the past and the future. We will learn to ride the horse through time. It is a sacred journey.

This meditation exercise will help you explore the past and the future. We can return to the past to resolve issues, and we can open to the future to see how the past and present are affecting what will unfold within our life. Its mythic imagery will stimulate dream activity, especially when performed sometime in the evening or before going to sleep. Even if you fall asleep during this exercise it will often stimulate dreams of the past when performed for three days in a row. It can also stimulate prophetic dreams of the future. The people and places within the dream scenario provide clues.

As in all meditations, music and fragrances can enhance the effects. One of the most effective aids for this exercise is the drum. Drums are connected to the heartbeat of the earth and are very important to incorporate in this shaman-type journey for the best results. Drumming helps the shaman to enter tan expanded state of consciousness. It is a tool for sacred journeying into the dreamtime and other realms.

The drumbeat should be slow and steady, and the participants should allow the drumbeat to lead them. Riding the drumbeat to the dream world is part of all shaman experiences. With practice it is easy to allow the drumbeat to escort you to the inner realms. As children many of us tapped out the clippity-clop rhythm of horses on our thighs. This same rhythmic beat of the horses' hoofs is a powerful aid to this journey. Practice drumming the rhythm of hoofbeats, slowing to the rhythm of our heartbeat.

Individuals sometimes wonder if they are experiencing a true shaman journey. The difference between a meditation and a true journey is the depth of the experience. In the journey, we are actually in it, feeling it and experiencing it first hand. It also will not always follow a prescribed pattern. On the other hand, in meditation exercises, we often observe ourselves experiencing the situation or imagine how it should be experienced. Imaging practices and meditation exercises lead to an ability to immerse ourselves fully into the midst of the experience. We become part, rather than just playing a part. The meditation aspects lead us to the control and experience of true shaman journeys.

Make preparations before performing this exercise. You may wish to use a favorite fragrance – essential oil or incense. Make sure you will not be disturbed. Perform a progressive relaxation, sending each part of the body warm and relaxed thoughts and feelings. The more relaxed you are, the better it will work. If you are performing this before bedtime, read through the scenario several times so that it is firmly implanted in the mind. This way if you fall asleep during the process, it will still work for you through the dream state.

If you have a drum, use it. Begin the slow, steady, rhythmic drumbeat of horses hooves on the drum for about five minutes. Then gradually slow it down to the rhythm of the heart. Make sure it is slow and steady. Then close your eyes and imagine the following scenario:

You are standing in a green meadow. The sun is warm upon the body. In the distance is a great river. Then there is movement at the far end of the meadow. You hear the whinnying of a horse and you watch as a beautiful horse trots into view, head held high and its mane flowing. It looks at you, tosses its head and trots toward you.

It stops in front of you and the sunlight seems to shimmer off its strong body. Its eyes fix you and you realize that you know this horse. You are not sure from where, but you do know it. Its head bobs as if acknowledging your recognition and it moves over to a large boulder and stands next to it. It looks back at you and waits.

You realize that you are being invited for a ride. You slowly walk over and you stroke the horse gently. It is comforting and familiar. As you walk around, you are not sure if you should. But with each touch of the horse, your confidence grows. You stand up on the boulder and holding the horse's mane, you slide your leg over the side of the horse. It stands steady and strong. You are tense, afraid that the horse will bolt and you gently lower yourself onto its back. The horse stands steady.

You wrap your hands in the mane and as you settle onto the horse, it steps slowly away from the boulder. It's as if it knows your nervousness and is going out of its way to ease it. Soon you relax as the steady walk begins to relax you.

You let the horse take you and you soon realize that it is moving toward the river. As it approaches the river, you can see that it seems to flow forever. You cannot see the beginning or the end – just bends and turns.

The horse stands at the edge of the water and you look out into the eddies and current. As you do the sun flashes upon the surface and you see images of things going on in your life at the present. You see your home, your place of work, your school, your family and your friends. Images of projects, goals and even difficulties shimmer and flow by you in the current. You are filled with wonder at the sight.

You look upstream, and you see images of the past week, glimpses of the recent past on the surface of the water. Further upstream you see flashes of the more distant past, events that have affected your life and what you now are.

You begin to realize that this is the river of your life. It is the flow of what you have done and been throughout time. You realize that even further up stream, beyond what you can see are probably past lives that have flowed down into what you now are.

Then you look downstream, and you see things that will unfold in the next day or so. You see current projects being completed, problems being solved and even some possible difficulties. You know that if you follow the river downstream you will discover what is yet to be.

Your heart is filled with wonder. Then the horse shifts under you. You realize that it is waiting to be told which way to go – upstream or downstream. You realize that part of the horse's magic is to ride you into the past or the future – if you desire. The horse can take you along the river so that you can see in the water the flow of events in your life.

You are amazed. Such possibilities! You realize this will take some thought but what adventures there can be. You decide that you will explore some other time. For now it is enough to know that the past and future are open.

The horse seems to read your mind and turns. It heads back to the meadow and stands next to that boulder. Holding onto the mane, you slide off its back and onto the boulder. You step around to look at him, stroking his cheeks and rubbing his neck. You thank the horse for this gift and step back. The horse lifts its head and lopes off to the far end of the meadow. There it turns and whinnies at you and disappears until the next time.

The images begin to fade and you find yourself back where you first began this journey. You understand that in time you can ride this horse into the past or into the future, It is your guide for sacred journeys into time.

The Ghost Owl

Two major events were going on. First, I had written a new book. I was very excited about it. It was Animal-Speak. I hadn't heard from the publisher; the time frame for them to commit had run out. I was trying to decide whether to offer it to another publisher who had expressed an interest. Second, I was frustrated in my efforts to get my educational possession and rehab permits from US Fish & Wildlife and the State of Ohio for working with birds of prey. My mind wrestled with both of these, as I drove to my Kung Fu class.

At the exit off the highway, I spot two crows in a tree, hopping from branch to branch, raising a ruckus. They are harassing what appears to be a hawk. (Later I would realize the significance of the two crows and my own two worries at that time.) I pull off the edge of the exit ramp to watch. As I do, I am amazed to see that it is not a hawk they are harassing. It is a barn owl - what used to be called the ghost owl. Although I have handled barn owls at Brukner Nature Center, I have never seen one in the wild. I am thrilled at this, because they are endangered in Ohio.

I watch as one of the crows flies off and then back again, cawing repeatedly. Then the barn owl flies off. Its brilliant white chest flashed and the rust of its wing feathers stood out strong. It dipped soaring across the distant field and landed near the top of tree about a quarter mile away, its white shimmering. I knew this was important.

Over the next several months I began having dreams of the barn owl. In one dream I asked the barn out about helping with my federal and state permits working with birds of prey. Although there was no acknowledgment in the dream, I awoke knowing that the permit had been granted. I told my wife it would be in the mail the next day. The next day the mail arrived with a letter and a permit to possess and work with birds of prey.

Not long after this the barn owl appeared in my dreams again. It wasn't just a single barn owl; it was many barn owls. When I awoke, I knew that the contracts for my book would arrive in the mail the next day. And they did.

Over the years the barn owl returns occasionally to me. Mostly it is to let me know when important mail or communication is coming my way (usually the next day). Always it appears to let me know that spirit is listening and working with me.

Chapter 4

Hawk & Owl Medicine

How often have we heard such things as "He has the eyes of a hawk" or "She has the wisdom of an owl"? Birds of prey fascinate people. They are ancient symbols of power, strength and vision. They have a fierce beauty and a commanding presence. They are the hunters. They have abilities and strategies to hunt and survive successfully.

Raptors (from the Latin word to snatch or seize) are of two types. There are daytime hunters and nighttime hunters. The daytime birds of prey or raptors are hawks, falcons, eagles, osprey and more. The nighttime raptors are the owls.

Hawks are powerful, visionary and awe-inspiring. They see 8 times better than humans and they can soar, fly and strike with great speed. Owls are marvelous and mysterious. They are versatile vocalists – howling, screeching, trilling and hooting. They have extraordinary vision, amazing hearing, powerful beaks and silent flight.

Together they are the most amazing birds of prey. They are hunters and are very successful at it. Both hawks and owls have great singular focus. When they see a prey and pursue it, they do not take their eyes off of it. In fact they may have the most highly evolved eyesight of all living things. They see in color and black and white. They have the ability to see in poor lighting and some birds can even see into the ultraviolet range.

They have the ability to fly at great speeds and with sharp maneuvering. They have powerful talons to grab and kill prey. They have developed many hunting strategies and will often adapt them to the situation. Some of these include still hunting, high searching, stalking, flushing from cover, deception flights and more. They teach us how to adapt our own pursuits.

Birding Etiquette

Birding can be done in the city or the country. It can even be done in your own back yard. Whether seeking out a hawk, an owl or any other type of bird, there are certain preparations, courtesies and considerations to keep in mind.

Preparations:

1. Be prepared with a good field guide to identify the bird.
2. Equip yourself with a pair of binoculars. When using binoculars, remain looking at the subject and raise the binoculars to your eyes. You will be less likely to lose sight.
3. Wear comfortable clothes. Keep in mind that you may be sitting or standing for long periods of time.
4. If you choose to photograph, telephoto lens and extra film is always beneficial.

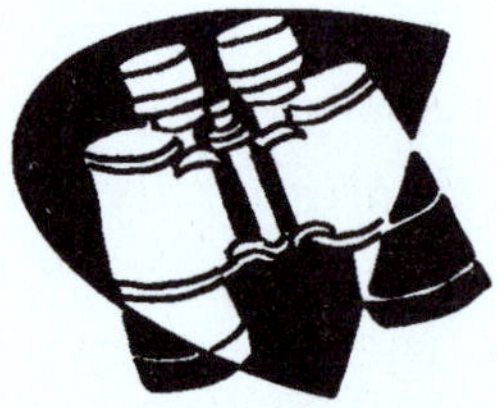

Etiquette:

1. Respect private property and "No Trespassing" signs.
2. Do not endanger or disturb the welfare of birds or other wildlife.
3. Avoid chasing or flushing birds.
4. Avoid using recordings to attract birds.
5. Remain a good distance from nesting areas and do not disturb nests and eggs.
6. Do not snap branches to get a more perfect photo. Many birds choose nesting sites that are particularly hidden by branches.
7. Remain as quiet as possible. In this way, if you disturb birds, they will usually return to normal activity within ten minutes of so.

Their feet are heavily scaled with powerful talons for gripping and killing prey. It is also their first line of defense. Some talons are specialized, as in that of the osprey. It has special pads to help it grasp and hold onto slippery fish.

It is tough to be a bird of prey though. Three out of every four hawks die before they are one year old. They do not learn to hunt properly. They fly into power lines. They get hit by cars while pursuing prey. And people still shoot them, which is illegal. If they live through that first year though, they will usually live to be an adult. When hawks appear at the beginning of new projects or endeavors, we should remember this. The first year will be difficult, but if we survive it, we will ultimately succeed.

People may not be able to tell the difference between a hawk or an eagle or an owl or a falcon, but they are able to recognize that it is a bird of prey. They sense the strength and the power of the bird. They realize it is not like what they normally see in their own back yards. Birds of prey arrouse a sense of awe. I have been very honored and blessed to work with these amazing animals for many years, and I am still amazed and in awe of them.

I present many educational programs every year in schools and to various organizations, and it is great fun to see the eyes widen as I pass among the students and young people with one of my hawks. Most have never seen a hawk or any other bird of prey up close. And once seen in this way, they are never looked at the same way again. I have found that if you create a memory, if you ignite a spark of wonder, their hearts will open to Nature forever. And hawks and owls stir the imagination and open the heart to wonder more easily than any other birds. It is a testament to their power, their magic and their medicine.

The Mysterious Owl

The owl is the silent guide. It has been worshipped and hated throughout the world, but always it intrigues and fascinates. It is the epitome of mystery, magic, vision and guidance. The owl is a creature of the night, and night symbolizes the darkness within – the places where great secrets and great treasures are hidden. The night is the place of our dreams and our fears. When owl appears dream activity will be intensified, bringing perspective and clarity to daily activities.

In the natural world, the owl is not the most intelligent of animals, and yet it is a powerful and instinctual creature that can teach us much. Its visual and auditory senses are tremendous, and so its appearance always reflects a heightening of our own senses – especially of the intuition. The owl's eyes are adapted to see the subtlest of movement with the least amount of light. Because of this, you will see subtleties that you may not have noticed before. Trust these impressions, whether they come during the day or at night because owls see very well during both times.

An owl's hearing is just as acute as its sight. Because of this, when owl appears, we will hear undercurrents in the voices of others. Trust what you do or do not hear in the conversations around you – no matter how strange you may think your impression is. When we learn to trust those instincts, then we see our own wisdom manifesting.

Owls fly silently. The front edges of their wings and feathers have a fringe, which quiets their flight. This facilitates the silent hunt, and thus when owl shows up, it is time to turn to our endeavors with silence. An old adage tells of how there is strength in silence. Never is this more significant than when the owl appears. Owls teach us to trust our instincts, the silent impressions. They provide guidance through heightening our senses. Their appearance always indicates that help and guidance are available to us, but it is still up to us to act upon it.

The owl is a powerful and aggressive hunter, with instincts that are honed for survival. Owl is a silent and aggressive hunter, and goals should be pursued in this same manner.

Are we ignoring our impressions? Are we pretending not to see what is apparent? Are we not listening closely enough to what others are saying and to what is going on around us? Are we letting others know of our intentions and actions too soon? Are we heeding our dreams and the insight they are providing? Are help and guidance available but being ignored? When owl appears, it always indicates a need to heed wise counsel – whether from our own instincts or from others around us. We need to step back, listen and watch before we act.

The Magnificent Hawk

The hawk is one of the most amazing raptors. Universally, they have been recognized as guardians and messengers. There are many species of hawks, and even when people cannot recognize the particular species, they are able to recognize it as a hawk. Buteos are soaring hawks with broad wings and accipiters are faster with narrowed wings and rarely found soaring. All hawks see 7-10 times better than humans. In fact, if a hawk could read and if a newspaper was held up at one end of a football field while the hawk was at the opposite, it could easily read the headlines. Because of their vision and strength, all hawks are guardians.

Hawks spend three-fourths of their day perched somewhere observing the area around them. They are able to detect the subtlest of movements. It patiently waits until the best moment to strike. Because of this the appearance of a hawk can alert us to possibilities for new ventures and possible trouble. The hawk's appearance tells us that there is protection in the ventures we are embarking upon, and that our own perceptions will be heightened through the process. We must learn to trust in them.

The powerful beak and talons of the hawk are other outstanding characteristics. They have great ability to grasp without fear, and its appearance now reminds us to grasp our own opportunities when they present themselves. Hawks have a scaled leg to protect themselves against bites when striking upon its prey. It is a reminder that there is protection for the things we strike out for.

Hawk's appearance always heralds a time of greater strength and vision, which will help us tremendously in our present endeavors. We will have protection in our journeys and endeavors. Now is the time to gallantly move forward with them.

Three out of every four hawks born every year will die before they are one year old. It is tough to be a raptor. Those that do survive their first year will usually live to be adults. When hawk appears, it can indicate that there may be many complications and difficulties in our endeavors at this time. It can warn that the first year of what we are embarking upon will be most difficult, and thus we should try to look ahead to anticipate and head off as many problems as possible. We are likely to meet some strong opposition. Impatience will create problems in our undertakings. If we are patient and persist, we will ultimately succeed.

When hawk appears, we should ask ourselves some questions. Are we looking ahead to possible problems? Are we protecting ourselves appropriately? Are we being impatient in our endeavors? Are striking out too strongly right now when we should be sitting and observing what is going on around us? Are we heeding our own inner vision?

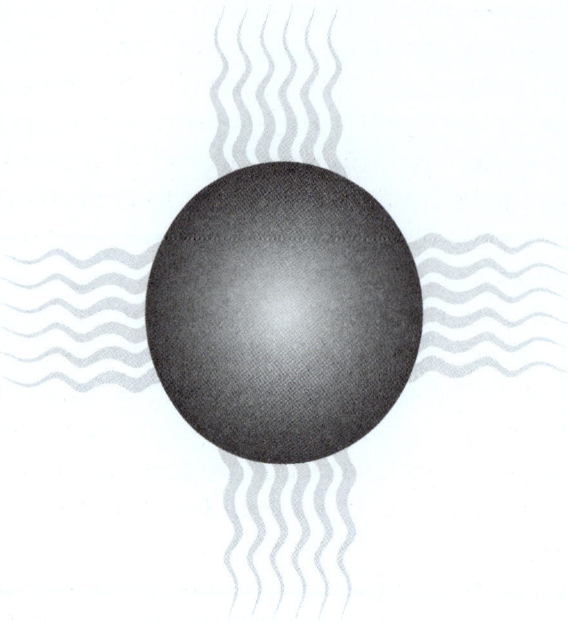

Sun & Moon

No bird has had as much myth about it as the owl. It has been both devil and saint. It has been something to fear and something to bless. In Greece it was associated with the goddess Athena. It has come to be associated with magic, mystery and things of the night.

The hawk has had its myths as well. It is a bird of healing to the Pueblo people. To the Ojibwa it is a bird of vision. In Greek mythology it was associated with Mercury.

The hawk is a daytime bird; the owl is night time. The hawk is solar and the owl is lunar. The hawk is yang and the owl is yin. Together they bring balance. They bring the night into the day and the day into the night. When we work with hawk, we will also work with owl and vice versa. They often share the same territory. When one appears it is always good to explore its counterpart. They are opposites that balance each other.

Red-Tailed Hawk	Great Horned Owl
Red-Shouldered Hawk	Barred Owl
Broad Winged Hawk	Barred Owl
Kestrel	Screech Owl
Harrier Hawk	Short-Eared Owl
Gyrfalcon	Snowy Owl

Dictionary of Hawks and Owls

Barn Owl

Keynote: listen to what is not said, spirit communication and assistance, elimination of pests and problems

When farmers went out to their barns at night, a white form flying overhead often surprised them. Many thought it was a ghost but it was usually just a barn owl. Because of this though, the barn owl is also known as the ghost owl.

The barn owl has a heart shaped disc face. It has a white underbelly with golden buff feathers on top. It is an owl that connects us to old spirits and the energy of old haunts.

The barn owl is one of the most exquisite owls. It is the master mouser. It can locate its prey from a subtle sound in pitch dark, swiveling its head to pinpoint the location. It even employs a kind of echolocation. A pair of nesting barn owls can eliminate more mice per night than ten cats together. Barn owls are inventive opportunists, and if need be, they will hunt by day or by night. They will take advantage of the opportunities.

Although all owls see well at night (and during the day), it is the barn owl's hearing that is most special. A large portion of its brain is devoted to sorting out and identifying and locating sounds. When barn owls appear, listen to what is not being said. Remember that spirit is trying to communicate with us and will help us eliminate pests and solve problems. There is spirit help available for us.

Burrowing Owl

Keynote: priestlike responsibilities; links to the spirits and to the underworld; keep sense of humor in regards to things spiritual

The burrowing owl is very different from most species of owls. Even from a mythical aspect, its significance is often ambiguous. Among the Pueblo peoples, the burrowing owl is one of seven owls, of which only three are treated with any special importance: the screech owl, the great horned owl and the burrowing owl.

All owls have had many misconceptions and legends about them. They have been associated with life and death. They have been thought of as the reincarnation of the dead and a sign of fertility and pregnancy. Many people placed an owl feather in the bed of a baby to help it sleep during the day.

To the Pueblo, the burrowing owl knew how to chase away clouds and rain. It had learned how to do this to prevent its burrow from being flooded. When rains were flooding its home, the owl forced the tip beetle to disgorge its terrible smell into a bag. Then the owl drummed, beating on the bag, releasing the smell into the air, chasing away the rain clouds.

While most owls are nocturnal, the burrowing owl is very active during the day. It is often found nesting in the burrows of other animals, and it most frequently shares its habitat with prairie dogs. For those to whom the burrowing owl appears, the prairie dog should also be studied, as it is one of your totems as well.

The Zunis labeled the burrowing owl as "The Priest of the Prairie Dogs". When the burrowing owl appears there will arise occasions in which we find ourselves having to assume the role of priest or priestess in some area of life. This may be formal or it may be informal, as in the case of increasingly providing spiritual guidance.

It also has a habit of nodding and bobbing around, sometimes very theatrical displays. Thus it sometimes fluctuated between the image of a priest and that of a clown. Because of this it is a reminder of our need to keep our sense of humor – especially about things in the spiritual realm. Often as I travel and teach, I encounter people who are so serious about their "spiritual path", that they actually put people off. They seem to be lost in the misconception of long suffering and martyrdom as the path to spirituality. Humor is essential life and health, and nowhere is it more essential than in our spiritual activities. If we have lost our ability to see the humor in ourselves and our life path, it is time for a change. The burrowing owl is a reminder not to take ourselves so seriously. We should always retain the ability to poke a little fun at our path and ourselves. It keeps us grounded and it keeps the ego in check.

While most owls nest in trees, the burrowing owl is a ground dweller, usually living underground. Because of this, it is often a connection to the dead and the darkness – the underworld. A more substantial connection with spirits will be occurring. This is also a further reminder to keep us grounded and down to earth in our spiritual activities, studies and explorations. The spiritual path is not one that leads up into some blinding light into which all of our troubles are dissolved. Rather it is a path that leads to finding the light within and shining out into our world.

Cooper's Hawk
Keynote: patience, speed and accuracy

The Cooper's Hawk is often confused with its smaller cousin the sharp shinned hawk. They often share the same territory and although the sharp shinned is smaller, when viewed singly, it is difficult to tell one from the other. The biggest difference is in the shape of the tail feathers. The Cooper's hawk has more rounded tail feathers, while the sharp shinned are sharper and straighter across.

The Cooper's hawk is a well-proportioned combination of size, color and form and it is often found in deciduous forests. It mainly hunts small to medium sized birds, sitting patiently in a tree for hours, waiting to spot its prey. Then it maneuvers closer until the last minute when it flies and strikes with amazing speed. It prefers to hunt in fairly open areas, watching for prey from an inconspicuous spot.

When the Cooper's hawk appears, it is a sign to be patient and watch. Look for the right moment to act and when it presents itself, do so with great speed. Don't be afraid to maneuver closer to your goal (as inconspicuously as possible) before striking.

Goshawk

Keynote: skillful and relentless pursuit and maneuvering

The goshawk is the largest North American accipiter. Hawks are often divided into two common groups - accipiters and buteos. While buteos are soaring hawks, accipiters are fast flying birds with smaller wings. The goshawk's wings are long for an accipiter. It is a large bird of prey that looks similar to the American kestrel.

The goshawk is found in northern and mountain forests. It is primarily a bird eater, and even though its wings are large, it is an extremely skillful flyer, with a skillful ability to pursue prey through heavily wooded areas.

The goshawk is usually a gray hawk with a white eye stripe. This ghostlike hawk maneuvers with the grace of spirit. It often indicates new spirit contact within our life that will provide guidance in accomplishing our goals and maneuvering through any troubled waters that will appear or are already stirred up within our life. This magnificent hawk shows us the power of our own spirit, and reminds us of our ability to achieve our hopes and dreams. It is always a message: "Remember who you truly are."

Individuals for whom this bird appears must trust in their own ability to maneuver in all that is going on. Planning maneuvers may not work. This is a time to trust your instincts in the correct moves. Trust in spirit at this time, but remember that spirit just directs. It is your efforts that must be employed.

Goshawks prey on a variety of small mammals and birds. This includes pheasants, squirrels, pigeons and even the occasional fox. They often concentrate their hunting on the most plentiful prey in the area. Goshawks remind us to seek a variety of things to feed ourselves, physically and spiritually. They also remind us that often we must focus on what is most plentiful at the time and not ignore it for that which may not be as plentiful or accessible.

When the goshawk appears we should ask ourselves some important questions. Are we afraid to pursue what is available to us at this time? Are we not trusting in our own power of spirit? Are we giving up the pursuit too quickly? Goshawk reminds us that if we can dream it, we can achieve it.

Great Horned Owl

Keynote: assert; become more aggressive; power of silence

The great horned owl is probably the most powerful bird of prey in our country. It is strong, aggressive and can very easily snap the neck of a woodchuck. It will even take on other birds of prey. About the only other bird of prey that could hold its own against it is a golden eagle and it would be a toss of the coin to see who would come out on top. This powerful owl attacks life with a fervor and reminds us to do the same.

The great horned owl is named for the feathers that stick up on its head. They are not really horns, and neither are they ears. They are just tufts of feather whose purpose is still unknown.

The favorite food of this owl is the skunk and this is primarily because the owl has no sense of smell. (This is particularly helpful if you are going to be eating skunk.) Like all owls, it has a fringe on its feathers, enabling it to fly silently. In this way it is more able to prey upon nocturnal mammals such as the skunk. It is a reminder to be silent in our pursuits for the greatest success. Do not be letting everyone know of your activities.

All owls open us to the mysteries and power of the night – a time of facing fears and giving birth. The great horned owl reminds us to aggressively pursue what we wish.

Gyrfalcon

Keynote: sacred gift and knightly codes; slow & steady brings fastest progress

The gyrfalcon is the largest and one of the most majestic of all falcons. It is found in the Arctic tundra, almost solely in Canada, Northern Europe and Scandinavia. It is well adapted to this northern climate. It does not migrate, keeping to the harsh environment even in winter. Its belly feathers are long enough to keep its feet warm.

Its favorite food is the Arctic hare, but it will also hunt ptarmigan, lemmings and sea birds. It nests on rock ledges, reflective of its closeness to spirit. This gives it a wider vision. When the gyrfalcon appears our own intuitive and spiritual vision will grow, especially in perceiving opportunities and the best paths to progress.

It has ancient and sacred ties to spirit. The name is thought to come from the slang Latin, meaning "sacred falcon". In olden times, it was considered a knightly gift in falconry.

It has two primary forms, a white and dark form. The dark form has two tones with a dark hood. The white form has a regal coloring that has been compared to the back of a snow leopard. It shares many of the same qualities, and thus studying the snow leopard can provide some insight.

The gyrfalcon has wing beats that are slow and deep, but they produce a deceptively rapid flight. This slow deep movement also helps it to conserve energy in a climate where food may not be as readily available. The gyrfalcon teaches how to be conserve and steady our movements for the fastest progress.

This is the bird of the knight's quest - regardless of that quest. It is a reminder to keep the knightly code sacred at this time for our greatest benefit. When the gyrfalcon appears, there is a sacred gift about to come into our life. Our efforts and code of behavior will be rewarded. Though our progress may have been slow, it is about to accelerate.

Harrier Hawk
Keynote: spirit messages, staying grounded when working with the psychic

The harrier is a hawk of the marsh and wetland areas. Like many falcons, it has a dark hooded head. Also like falcons it is an extremely gifted flyer - fast and skilled at aerobatics

The harrier is most active at dawn and dusk. These are sacred times, intersections in the worlds and dimensions - neither morning nor neither night. These are times when the veils between the physical and spiritual are thinner and the doors between these dimensions are more open. Thus the harrier is always an indication of spirit messages - often from a family member who has passed on, frequently of the opposite sex.

This is further reinforced by two facts. Its indigenous environment is the marsh and wetlands. These are also sacred places - "Tween Places", where the physical and spiritual intersect more intensely. Marshlands are neither entirely water nor land. They are in-between.

The male during mating performs great aerobatic feats to impress the female. It loops and dives, displaying its skills to court the female. The harrier nests on the ground, and during the nesting the male hunts for the female and the young, fulfilling responsibilities to its family unit. The female harrier prefers mammals, while the male prefers birds.

This is a strong reminder that when we work with the less substantial realms we must stay grounded. We can work with the spirit but we must live in the physical. That is where our responsibilities lie. We must stay grounded when we work with the psychic and spiritual worlds. No matter how skilled we may be, we must stay grounded and fulfill our responsibilities, take care of our daily obligations.

Harris Hawk

Keynote: cooperative pursuit and hunting

A number of years ago, a falconer in Colorado by the name of Kin Quitugua took me on one of his Hawkquest educational programs. His primary birds were Harris Hawks, which he used to hunt and to educate the public. He also used them to help rehabilitate releasable birds of prey. At the time he was using his hawks to help teach a golden eagle how to hunt. He allowed me to fist his bird CC and I was so amazed at the behavior of his hawks that I almost forgot to release her during the demonstration. One would fly from above to scare out the rabbits, while the other came from below. This cooperative hunting technique is unique among birds of prey, and it is the primary lesson of this species. They teach cooperation for the greatest success.

Harris hawks are not loners like so many birds of prey. They breed in small groups and hunt in teams. Then they share the prey. Their hunting parties are usually family groups. The group hunting is an adaptive behavior. Harris hawks live in desert areas where prey is often larger than in other environments. It is also more scarce. So in order to survive as a species group hunting was adopted over the years.

One of their more amazing behaviors is their stack perching. In the desert there are few trees to perch on, and so the Harris hawks will often stand and perch on each other shoulders on top of a cactus.

When the Harris hawk appears, it is time to get help from like-minded individuals. Larger goals are best accomplished with the assistance of others. Bigger goals will be accomplished more effectively if we do not try and do it all ourselves. Are you trying to do everything yourself? Do you need to let others help? Are you or others around you being uncooperative?

Reassess your goals. As with all hawks, Harris hawks have tremendous vision, and they are able to see larger prey and goals. Trust in your vision, but also trust in others' abilities to help you accomplish the goals. It will benefit everyone when there is cooperation and working together.

Long-Eared Owl

Keynote: silent and assertive defense

The long-eared owl is a slender, medium-sized, grayish owl. Like the great horned owl, it also has feather tufts, but longer. Thus its name. The feather tufts are close together and directly over the facial discs of this owl. No one is truly sure what purposes the tufts serve. Theories vary from the idea that it is for courtship appearance to threatening displays to camouglage.

The long wings of this owl give a large appearance when in flight, but the flight is very graceful. Individuals to whom the long-eared owl appears often have deceptive appearances, being much more creative and productive than believed. They are often indications of a need to focus on the creation and protection of endeavors rather than the environment in which endeavors taking place. The grace and recognition will come in time.

It is a "fly by night" owl, never building its own nest, but rather using deserted squirrel and crow nests, but it is still a powerful parent. The long-eared owl is fierce in defending its young. It is also presents a great "wounded bird act" to draw away intruders.This bird tells us that it is not the place where we give birth that is important but that we do and defend what we give birth to fiercely. It is a sign that protection of our creative endeavors is most important.

Even among owls this one is even more seldom seen. It is extremely nocturnal, and during the day remains quiet and very well hidden. Nocturnal birds and animals usually reflect a tremendously active dream life from which comes great inspiration. This is especially true of the long-eared owl. When this bird appears, nighttime is going to be a more productive and creative time.

Merlin

Keynote: quick and magical maneuvers and shapeshiftings

Merlins, like the mythical character, are magical birds. The merlin is a "pigeon hawk". Actually a member of the falcon family, it has a slate blue crown and black back, and mimics the flight of pigeons to sneak up on unwary prey. It also will use its flying maneuvers to startle flocks of birds and then in seemingly magical displays of flying, it snatches stragglers from the air.

Its ability to mimic pigeons in order to capture prey, is an indication of what the message of this bird is. Sometimes we must appear as something we are not in order to capture what we need or want. It weaves a little shapeshifting magic, creating an illusion in order to accomplish its goals.

The merlin can also appear if we need to look for someone around us who may not be what he or she appears to be. We may find ourselves in a vulnerable position and should be cautious about becoming someone's prey.

The merlin in falconry was a preference of noble ladies. The merlin is easily trainable and was then often returned back to he wild after a season of hunting. Because of this, the merlin is a reminder to weave and use a little magic for the time being. It is an indication of new - and often temporary - doors of learning will open. We should take advantage of these opportunities, undertake some quick training, and in order to accomplish what we need at the moment. The learning will come quickly and will serve its purpose for the time.

Are others around you appearing, as something they are not? Are we doing all we can to help ourselves? Are we using our magic inappropriately? Are we not using the magic that we should? Are we allowing ourselves to be vulnerable? Now is the time to shapeshift our life and ourselves a little for the greatest benefits.

Osprey

Keynote: assertive hunting and actions

Often mistaken for immature bald eagles, the osprey is a fish hawk. It has an eye stripe or a dark facial mask. The osprey, like the eagle, has a head of white feathers. Unlike the bald eagle, it usually has a white breast as well. It is found near water and coastlines. It is the only raptor with a reversible outer toe for an extra firm grip and its footpads have spicules for grasping slippery fish. It is a bird of prey that teaches us how to grasp and hold onto what we go after. Osprey is a sea hawk. To the Pueblo people it was known as a water eagle. It is more skillful at diving into water and catching fish than the bald eagle.

It builds a huge stick nest. Some can weigh up to 1/2 ton. It uses a shrill whistle and defends its nest aggressively against intruders., even against other ospreys that hunt in its territory. In competition for a mate, they perform amazing and frightening feats. They will lock talons with other osprey and they will do a freefall spin until one or the other breaks away

The osprey sometimes submerges completely under the water to capture fish. It has an enlarged cere that can cover its nostrils in water. The diving into waters to grasp food can be symbolic of diving into the creative waters of life to awaken and draw forth that, which will nourish us.

The courtship ritual is powerful. The male performs a fish dance, flying up and down in front of the female, bringing fish to her. This is done to demonstrate to the female what great providers they are.

When the osprey appears, it is time to check our commitments to those people and things closest to us and the of commitment of others to us. Remember that ospreys are active hunters. Are we truly going after what we desire? Are we giving it our all? Are we diving in or hooding back? How far are we willing to go to achieve what we seek?

Red-Tailed Hawk

Keynote: vision and protection, adaptability

The red-tailed hawk is the most common and adaptable hawk in the United States. It is due to its adaptability that its numbers grow strong while other birds of prey diminish. It has been a symbol of strength and great vision wherever it is found. During the fall of its second years, the eyes of the red-tail darken and the feathers begin to molt to the reddish brown colors, from which it gets its name. This color reflects the powerful creativity available.

To the Pueblo it was known as the red eagle. Its feathers were sacred in healing ceremonies. These hawks have a great ability to soar and glide but it spends three-fourths of its day perched somewhere, overlooking an area. This reflects its confidence and ability to accomplish tasks easily and fully. When they appear, your confidence should rise and people will begin to notice.

They have tremendous eyesight, seeing 8-10 times better than humans. They teach us to trust in our vision of things coming our way. The sky is the realm of the red-tailed hawk. Through its flight it communicates to us and aligns us with the great creator spirit. It opens our visionary abilities and stimulates new energy for our unique life purposes.

Screech Owl

Keynote: fierce individuality; cooperate to succeed

Screech owls are one of the smaller owls in existence. They usually come in two colors, gray and red. Like the great horned owl, they have tufts of feathers on top of their head. They are often mistaken as baby great horneds. Most often the sounds heard from them are a trilling or a whinny sound. If threatened, then the screech is heard.

Like all owls though, they are aggressive hunters. Sometimes they use cooperative hunting, with several members working together. This ability to cooperate to survive sets them apart from other owls. And still they maintain a fierce individuality. They remind us that we do not lose our own individuality when joining in a cooperative venture. We increase our chances for success while remaining independent. Screech owls are the most sociable of all owls. Sometimes they live in small groups of 3-4. Again this reinforces the idea of cooperation for greatest success.

Sharp-Shinned Hawk

Keynote: vision, perception and action; impeccable timing

The sharp-shinned hawk is one of several hawks often found within the cities and suburbs. It is an accipiter, a woodland hawk with short wings and long tails., distinguished from its soaring relatives the buteos which have broader and longer wings and shorter tails. The short rounded wings give it great maneuverability in woodlands. Because of this it often reminds us that we will be able to maneuver through the situations going on around us with much greater ease than we may have imaged. This hawk is very quick flyer, and it will often come into yards to prey on small birds. It darts through trees, across lawns and will seize an unwary bird, carrying it off in its talons.

Among the Pueblo it was considered a lesser hawk, but being swift and tireless, it served as an inspiration for youths. It was a relative of Kisa, a Hunting Hawk deity of the Hopi. In one of their legends it gives to the Hopi the throwing stick or boomerang with magical qualities for hunting small prey. The stick was modeled after its curved wing.

As with all hawks, it has excellent eyesight, seeing about seven times better than humans. It is fast and agile flyer and thus when it appears it helps us to see opportunities and reminds us to act quickly to take advantage of them. The appearance of the sharp-shinned often reminds us to act.

The sharp-shinned hawk lays its eggs with a unique sense of timing. They are laid so that the fully-fledged young leave the nest in time to practice their hunting skills on the young of small songbirds and other small species of birds. This sense of opportune timing is often found among those who have the sharp-shinned hawk as a totem. They have a knack for timing activities appropriately and most beneficially.

If the sharp-shinned hawk has appeared, we should ask ourselves some questions. Are we not pursuing strong enough that which has presented itself to us? Are we not looking far enough ahead? Are we hesitating to act? Remember that timing is everything. This hawk is a tireless and agile hunter, and it reminds us to act on the opportunities we perceive.

Short-Eared Owl
Keynote: aggressive pursuit of skills and goals

The short-eared owl is a tawny, medium-sized owl. It has piercing yellow eyes. It is extremely adept at head rotation. All birds though do have extra vertebrae in the neck, giving them the ability to rotate as much as 270 degrees and even a bit more. The short-eared owl though is extremely adept at this, enhancing its alertness and perception. This is probably so as it is - unlike the majority of owls - a daytime hunter. It hunts also at night, but mostly during the day. Its medicine or power is active both day and night.

It shares the marshes with the harrier hawks and as skilled a flyer as the harrier may be, the short-eared owl is even more skilled. The two can sometimes be observed chasing each other as if involved in good-natured flying competitions. Individuals with a short-eared owl as a totem usually have a friend / competitor in an important role within his or her life. A study of the harrier hawk is also important and will benefit you.

While the great blue heron often is considered the king of the marshlands, it is the short-eared owl that can truly rule it. They are aggressive and fiery. Their scientific name is Asio Flammeus, and it has flamelike markings, reflecting their fiery personality. The short-eared owl roosts and nests on the ground. It is unique among owls in that it will meticulously build its home. This is often an indication of a need to develop your skills and talents meticulously. Build your life solidly, taking the time to do so correctly. Develop your life skills consciously.

Snowy Owl
Keynote: prophecy and spirit

Snowy owls are magnificent, daytime owls. Larger than the great horned, it is known for its snowy white appearance. It can hunt in full sunlight or complete darkness, and it has the unique ability to adjust its iris to allow varying degrees of light to pass through. Learning to focus and use the eyes, is what allows us to open more fully to other dimensions. The snowy owl can reveal the presence of spirit and open us up to prophecy.

This owl hunts by sitting and waiting. It is a bird of patience, and reminds us to be patient as well. We must trust that what we need is coming. This trust comes from knowledge of the future. This is a bird of prophecy and its appearance reminds us to trust in our own destiny. We will have what we need.

The snowy owl has an uncanny knack for moving to places where food will be plentiful. It seems to be able to predict possible famine areas and moves long before they hit. They help us to be more opportune in our actions. They awaken within us that prophetic instinct.

Skill
Development

How To Spot An Owl

Benefits:

- **Increases awareness of the presence of owls**
- **Expands all perceptions**
- **Develops sensitivities to the natural world**

Most owls are nocturnal animals and thus they are not seen that often. They are also very well camouflaged, making it even more difficult. It is much more common to hear an owl than it is to see one. To see an owl at any time is a powerful sign that the owl is a messenger for you. To see an owl in the daytime is a thumping on the head of the importance of the owl to you and your life at this time.

Finding and actually seeing an owl is difficult, even after years of successfully seeking them. There are things that can be done though to help you locate owls.

1. Find out information about the owls in your area. Seek out areas where they are more likely to be found.

2. Use owl time to help you find them.

The hour just before dusk and just after are the times when owls are often most visible. They are moving from the inner woods to the outer edges to prepare for a night of hunting. For example, Great horned owls are crepuscular. This means they are most active and visible at dawn and dusk. They can often be seen silhouetted at forest edges at these times. They often perch on treetops and telephone poles.

3. Learn to recognize the silhouette form.

An owl's silhouette will appear headless – like a large lump. With hawks there is a silhouette of a head on a square, upright body.

4. Listen to the calls of the owl from different vantage points to determine a more specific location of the owl's nest.

Then in daylight hours try to find the nest. Move into that area quietly. Look for stick nests and pay attention to movement, crows and blue jays gathering and calling in that area. Take quiet walks through the woods, placing feet carefully. Stop frequently and look around. Pay attention to the trees and look for anything out of place – stick nest, holes in the tree trunks, a feather. Always move slowly and carefully. Look for cavities. Screech owls are natural cavity nesters.

5. When out seeking owls, move quietly and only speak in whispers. They have incredible hearing.

6. Pay attention to alarms set off by smaller birds.

Owls are great predators and many birds will scold and sound off the alarm to alert others to the predator. Crows cawing, jays scolding and birds gathering with a ruckus can be the sign of a predator bird.

7. Look for visible signs.

Owls and hawks will leave a whitewash (owl and hawk waste product) on trees they use regularly for roosting and eating. The whitewash is a cakey white and covers a large area. At the base of whitewashed trees, look for pellets. These are small regurgitated fur and bone in a small oval shaped wad that was indigestible.

8. When you find an owl, be still and quiet. Lower yourself toward the ground so that you appear less threatening.

Skill
Development

How To Spot A Hawk

Benefits:

- **Improves observation skills**
- **Strengthens awareness of hawk presence**
- **Strengthens awareness of the hawk guardianship**

Hawks are daytime animals. Because this is a much more active time for most humans, it is much easier to spot hawks around us. Hawks are also common to all environments – including urban and rural areas. They also spend much of their day perched, watching the area around them for prey. Many species are open field hunters, making them even more accessible to view.

I have worked with hawks for many years. I hold state and federal permits to work with them. My wife and I are often called to rescue injured hawks and owls. We possess our own hawks, which we use in dozens of educational programs every year. And the more we work with them, the more amazed we are by them. We have developed an unconscious habit of always looking for them. As a result we see them perched and we see them in flight. We hear their calls and we marvel at their dives.

Once you begin to look for and notice them, you will start seeing them everywhere. You will probably wonder why you didn't see them before. You will soon realize that they are constant reminders of the guardianship that is always around, whether seen or unseen.

There are some simple things that can be done to start locating hawks around you..

1. Find out information about the hawks in your area. Seek out areas where they are more likely to be found.

The edges of open fields are a common place. One of the easiest hawks to see is the red-tailed. It is one of the most common hawks across the country. It is usually seen out in the open.

2. The best times of the year are late fall, winter and early spring.
Tree foliage is less at these times of the years and it makes them more visible to the naked eye.

3. Look for their silhouette at the edges of fields and open areas.
They are usually perched high at the edges of fields which provide good hunting for them. Their silhouette will be of a head on as broad, somewhat square shouldered shape, perching upright overlooking open areas.

4. Hawks often perch atop telephone poles and billboards along highways.
On every trip I take I count the hawks that I see, and I always see some. The number helps provide insight into the energy and success of the trip.

5. Red-tailed hawks will occasionally soar among vultures.
Look for flashes of orangish colors as they soar above when the sun hits them.

6. Listen for their screech – especially in the spring.
Spring is the mating season and there are often aerial displays and a great deal of hawk-screeching going on. They are very vocal during the mating season or when other hawks come into their territory. When we first moved onto our farm, I had taken my two hawks out of the aviary and was weathering them on an outside perch so they could receive even more direct sunlight. It wasn't long before I was hearing screeching through my office window. I looked out and I saw that a mated pair of red-tails had come out of the woods and were raising a ruckus about my hawks in their territory.

7. When you spot a hawk while walking through fields, be still and quiet.
Lower yourself toward the ground so that you appear less threatening. Remember that the hawk has probably seen you long before you see it. Move in a little closer, keeping your eye on it. If it begins to fidget and move a bit, stop and go no further, or you will flush it out and away.

The Honoring

I was in Florida teaching and lecturing. Whenever I am touring in Florida I rise early and go to the beach to greet the sun and meditate in the early morning. It is peaceful and rejuvenating.

I walked into the water about waist deep, reflecting on how great the tour was going. People were responding wonderfully to the workshops. My schedule was full. My how-to books were really begining to sell. I was beginning to think that maybe I would be able to make a living working and teaching in the spiritual field.

As I stood there in the water, I found myself humming softly, just enjoying the moment. As I did, small fish began swimming and jumping around me. When I stopped humming in amazement at them, they stopped and moved off. When I began humming again, they returned. This went on for about ten minutes and then I stopped, filled with wonder. I gave thanks to the Mother Waters for her sharing this with me, and as I completed my prayer, six to eight fish jumped at once in front of me, coming out of the water like a fountain.

I returned to the beach and sat down on my towel, lifting my face to the sun rising across the horizon. At the edge of the water stood a large Native American facing the ocean. His arms were raised up, palms to the sky. He wore a headress of feathers which looked like a sun disc behind his head. The rising sun made his feathers shimmer with color. He lowered his arms and he turned to look at me. A group of pelicans flying overhead, dipped down to greet him and then soared off. He nodded and then faded into the bright sunlight.

Since that day I have always remembered to give honor and thanks for my encounters and blessings.

Chapter 5

Bird & Feather Magic

Humans have always celebrated and marveled at the wonder of birds. Of all the animals, they are the most accessible to us. We have all experienced birds personally. They sing and call and we can hear them. They fly and perch and we can see them. But the truth is though that most humans pay little attention to the presence of birds, even though most societies at one time or another taught that all birds were messengers with some symbolic associations to them.

Birds were often considered the closest relatives to humans because they walk around on two legs like humans. Because birds move between the earth and the heavens, they were also universally considered divine messengers for us humans. They are the couriers of our prayers and wishes. Birds are powerful wish bringers and their powers were often invoked in ceremony and ritual through the use of feathers.

Bird feathers have often been signs to humans, and they can be tools of communication from us to the gods and other abstract spirit forces. Bird feathers have magical properties, and they can be used in healing, protection, spirit communication and prayers.

Birds are some of the best spirit messengers to work with. They have the ability to move between worlds and thus open us to the spirit realm. They are sensitive to climatic changes and can help us recognize changes in the climate of our own life. They are sensitive to the subtlest of thoughts and can teach us how to use our thoughts to communicate and to create. Their feathers are invitations to explore new worlds and possibilities.

The Use of Feathers

Most birds are protected under the Migratory Bird Act. When it comes to possessing feathers and parts of migratory birds – especially birds of prey – it is illegal both on federal and state levels:

" No person shall possess, import, export, transport, sell, purchase, barter, or offer for sale, purchase or barter, any migratory bird, or the parts, nests or eggs of such birds, except as may be permitted under the terms of a valid permit issued pursuant to the provisions of this Part and Part 13, or as permitted by regulations in this Part of Part 20 (the hunting regulations)." (21.11 / Title 50, Code of federal Regulations, Part 21; Migratory Bird Permits)

In essence, all feathers that you find are usually from some migratory bird, the list of which is extensive. Concern and attention is usually only given to endangered birds and birds of prey (hawks, owls, eagles, falcons).

There are two common misconceptions about feathers as magical tools and fetishes:

1. The first is that you must have a particular type of feather to accomplish specific feather tasks. For example, you must have a down feather to truly get protection. This is not so. All feathers redirect the flow of air and so any feather can help redirect the flow of negativity around us. Down feathers just may do it a little more easily for you.

2. The second misconception is that you must have a feather of the bird to connect with the energies of the bird. This is a wrong. Any feather can be used to connect you to any member of the bird realm. You do not need a hawk feather to connect with hawks. It is illegal to possess feathers of birds of prey, especially eagles. An effective way around this is to paint or dye a chicken feather to the color and pattern of the eagle. It will connect you to the energies of the eagle and the act of creating this eagle feather establishes a magical and creative bridge between you and the eagle spirit. You can also obtain a wide variety of feathers at most craft stores, including ones that are easily painted to the color and patterns of eagle feathers.

The Power of Feathers

Most birds are designed for lightness, having hollow bones, which is essential to flight. There are, in fact, only a few birds that cannot fly. Birds also are distinguished from other groups of animals by their feathers, which facilitate this flight but also insulates and protects. They are actually specialized skin scales. Like the fur and scales of other animals, feathers serve a variety of purposes – from insulation to balance to flight.

Feathers are unique to birds and it is one of the marvels of engineering. Feathers are light, flexible and strong. Different feathers serve different functions for the bird. Contour feathers are the most common and they allow air to flow over the bird. They are usually small, blunt and fluffy. They make birds less resistant to air and help the birds to rise. They are especially helpful when opening to the energies of spirit and they are most effective in healing work as aura dusters and for smudging / cleansing rituals. They stimulate creative energies and their smooth flow within our life.

Down feathers are found beneath the coverts and are closest to the actual skin of the bird. They are insulators and protectors. I often recommend that an individual carry a down feather if they are going to be in an emotionally stressed situation. It will help make him or her less sensitive to the environment. Down feathers are also excellent to use in bird healing masks, as will be discussed later in this chapter.

Flight feathers are longer and stiffer and more smoothly shaped. The longer wing and tail feathers are good for helping us to control our journeys. They are also effective in opening to the guidance of spirits. They help us to make proper decisions and are effective as aids in shamanic journeying and astral travel.

Birds preen (clean and care) for their feathers meticulously. Many birds coat them with an oil that helps seal them from water, helping to keep them dry and warm. This protects them against exposure to outside elements and inclement weather. Their feathers help protect us against inclement weather in our life endeavors and activities.

When birds gift us with feathers, it is a reminder of all these things and more. It is a reminder that they are here to help us. It is an invitation to work with them if we desire. It is an expression of willingness to serve as a messenger for us. If we accept the feather, we open ourselves to great potential magic and power.

Inviting Bird Magic

Birds are found in all environments, and our own backyards are ideal for inviting them into our life. Because most birds molt several times throughout the year, this will increase opportunity to be gifted with feathers for healing and magical endeavors. But we must let them know that we are willing to work with them.

Creating an environment for birds and inviting them into that environment is the best way of letting them know that we wish to work with them, and it is quite easy to accomplish. Once birds discover a receptive yard, many will come back year after year. In exchange for an environment that is bird friendly, they will gift you with feathers from time to time that you will be able to use to awaken your own magic.

Set up a feeder station

Birds need food, water and protection, all of which you can provide in your own backyard. Different birds feed on different kinds of food. Use a variety of feeders and foods. Many birds are seedeaters and most wild birdseeds are relatively inexpensive. Set the feeder station up where you can easily observe without disturbing.

For the most part birds are routine oriented. They do the same things at about the same time. They feed, preen and bathe at about the same time and for about the same length of time. In this way you will be able to learn of their behaviors and understand their communications to you more easily.

Set up a water station

Birdbaths come in a variety of forms and can actually be anything that is nontoxic and holds water. You can also put in a small pond if you have the space. For the most part, water areas do not need to be deep. An area about 2 feet wide and 2-3 inches deep can be quite beneficial for a large number of birds. Birds are attracted to moving water and so fountains can also be quite attracting to birds.

Build nestboxes

Many species of birds have lost natural locales for nesting. Most often this is due to habitat destruction. Providing nestboxes is a way of attracting permanent residents. Most nurseries have a variety of nestboxes. Some of the more common are enclosed (single family dwellers) and condominium (multiple family dwellers) style. Regardless of the style, it should be placed at least 6 feet off the ground in a sheltered or secluded area. Birds may not move in immediately, and sometimes it is difficult to tell.

There were many nest boxes in the backyard of our farmhouse when we moved into it, but we never saw any activity in them. We wondered if we needed to move them. We figured that maybe the birds had never used them. As my wife and I walked around, she wondered out loud if the openings were large enough, and to demonstrate, she stuck one of her fingers inside. As she pulled it out, a bluebird flew out of the opening, startling both of us. Sometimes they take up residence without being observed.

Make a Bird Garden

With a little effort beyond feeders and nestboxes, you can turn your backyard into a wildlife habitat. Regardless of how you plan your haven, it should have three things – trees and shrubs for cover, natural plants for food and water for the birds to bathe in. Some dense vegetation provides shelter and natural nesting sites for birds. The plants should be native and should attract insects or provide nuts, berries or other fruit. Water can be in the form of birdbaths and ponds.

Honor Your Guests

If you invite birds directly into your environment, you are making a promise to be more active in your stewardship of animals and of them particularly. This involves more responsibility. Part of that responsibility is to provide an environment where risks are limited. Fresh food should be available regularly and food should be provided year round. The birds will come to expect your yard to be a food source for them. You should protect the birds, as much as possible from predators – the most common being cats. While you cannot do anything about the occasional hawk that takes a bird, simply spraying the stray cat with water will usually do the trick. Squirrels can also be troublesome. They are good at overcoming obstacles and will often eat all of the food. Squirrel-proof feeders are available.

People frequently ask me about the bird that flies into the window. It is estimated that millions of songbirds die as a result of flying into windows every year. Sometimes the bird suddenly panics and flies into it without looking. A lot of times it sees its own reflection and is confused by it or believes it is an intruder in its territory. This is especially true in the spring when mating and courtship abounds. Placing things on the window so that the reflection is less clear is usually the best way of handing this.

As you make an attractive environment for birds, you will find yourself observing amazing activities. They will demonstrate their personalities and their unique qualities, and in return they will gift you with the occasional feather and work with you as messengers.

Smudging and Aura Dusting

There is a field of energy surrounding the human body. It is called the aura, and it has an electro-magnetic aspect to it. There is a flow, a giving off and receiving of energies constantly. Because of this, every time we come in contact with other people and other energies, there is an exchange. We accumulate energy debris like a static cling.

Smudging and aura dusters are used to cleanse and sweep the aura free of this static. It allows for a healthier flow of our energy, and it helps prevent stress and imbalance from becoming locked into the body to manifest as a possible dis-ease.

Smudging is a process of sweeping the aura clean of negative energies. Cleansing incense is used. Among the Native Americans sage and sweetgrass is often burned. As it smokes a feather or group of feathers are used to gently sweep the cleansing smoke over the body, around a room or around doorways. It cleanses and protect the individual and the environment form negative energies.

Aura dusting is the sweeping of the aura to help smooth out the flow of energy in and around the body. It is most often used in healing rituals with or without smudging. The process is the same. Smudging and aura dusting can be done with a single feather or a group of feathers.

1. The feathers never touch the body.
In soft, sweeping motions, the feathers are brushed through the aura of the person, about 3-6 inches from the body. If smudging, the smoke is brushed over the body. It is like bathing in the cleansing smoke.

2. The entire body should be swept or smudged.
Start at the head and sweep down, sweeping the static out of the aura down to Mother Earth where it is converted into helpful energies for the earth. Do this front, back and sides, under the arms and the bottom of the feet. If there are places that you intuitively feel need extra sweeping and cleansing, return to that area. (Remember that birds awaken subtle inspiration. Trust in it.)

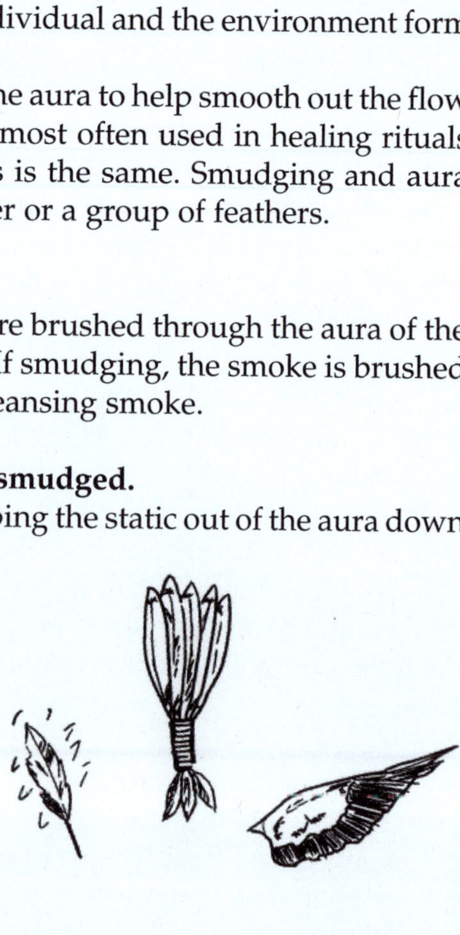

Feathers and Wish Making

Make a wish and blow out the candles. See a shooting star and make a wish. If a ladybug lights on you, make a wish. When it flies away, the wish will come true. Find and keep the first violet of spring and the fairies will work to make your wishes come true throughout the year. Upon your first look at a new moon, make a wish and within a year it will be fulfilled. Find a bluebird feather and a special wish will come true.

People make wishes for many things. Sometimes it seems as if people make up reasons just to make wishes. It is fun, but how many people actually believe that their wishes will come true?

Belief is necessary if wishes are to come true. The power of believing bridges our magical self to our outer self. It creates pathways of wonder and it is the blueprint for what we create in our lives. It bridges the inner to the outer, the mundane to the divine. Because of this, birds are the greatest allies in making wishes come true. They move from the earth to the sky and thus they are the experts at bridging worlds.

There's an old saying though: "Wishing will not get the cows milked." In other words, just wanting something to be will not make it so. But there are secrets to magical wishing. There is a skill to making things happen within our life. If we learn how to **work** with the magic of believing properly and learn to use one of the most powerful tools of wish making – *feathers* - the wishes we make will be fulfilled more often than we can even imagine.

So How Does It Work?

So how do we make our wishes come true? Is there a magical process for this? The answer is, "YES!" The magic of making wishes comes true is called **manifestation** and bird feathers can be a powerful tool to help bring it about. Manifestation is the process of making things happen, of bringing them into being. The process is both a magical and a practical one, and it affects everything in physical life. In order to make things happen – in order to have our wish-making work - we have to understand basics about energy.

Energy is both electrical and magnetic. We send out and draw to us energy by what we think, believe and do. If we wish to draw energies to us, we must send out the right message so that what comes to us is what we truly wish. The process of manifestation helps us with this.

If we wish to manifest anything - whether it's better health, more love, a new job, changes in our life or anything else - we must put energy into that process from all levels of our being. We are not just physical. We are also emotional, mental beings, and because of this we must put emotional and mental energy into this process as well.

We begin with mental energy. We are mental beings, and if we wish to manifest something – whether it's better health, more abundance or even greater love – we must put a mental energy into this magical process. We must imagine and visualize what it is we wish – as if it is already ours. Think of your mind as a magic wand. We must be specific about what we wish. Imagine it, picture it as if it is already yours and in as much detail as possible. Think of it as if you are picking something out of a catalog. You have chosen an item and now you are placing an order for it.

Next we must put in the emotional energy to make our wishes come true. The emotion though that we want to use is **not** desire. Desire – simply wanting or craving something – will not help bring it to us. It can actually hinder or block the process of having your wishes fulfilled.

If we think, "I really want that" or "I wish I had that now", there is an implied "but":

"I really want that, *but I can't have it.*"
"I wish I had that, *but I don't.*"

The implied "but" blocks or hinders the fulfillment of your wish.

The emotion we must put into this magical process is **anticipation**. We must anticipate that what we are imagining and visualizing is already on its way to us. It's as if we have placed that order from the catalog, and now we are waiting for UPS to drop it off at our front door. We have all had this emotion. Think back to one of your favorite holidays or birthdays as a young child. You knew you were going to get something. You didn't always know what it would be, but there was still an excitement. You anticipated a wonderful gift. This is the emotion we must try to generate.

Even if we put mental and emotional energy into this process, we must not forget the physical. We must put a physical energy into the process for it to work for us. Look at it this way. Imagine that you wish to have a new job. We begin by visualizing it in as much detail as possible. We picture all of the wonderful things that are ours now because of this job. Then we apply the emotional energy. We know the job is ours. We are excited about it. We know it is being offered; we know it is on its way. We are already celebrating its arrival in our life and all that we will have as a result of it.

But even if we have put forth the mental and emotional energy, if we do not do something in the physical to help bring it about, it will never manifest. We are physical beings and it is the physical part of the process that grounds and releases the mental and emotional to work for us.

In other words, even if we have visualized our new job, even if we anticipate its arrival, we must still prepare for it. We must prepare a resume, fill out applications, and do interviews. We must take appropriate physical actions to help or the job will never manifest. Our wish making will come to nothing. This is where the feathers come in.

Breathing Wishes into Feathers

We can use feathers to help ground the wish energy so that it is released more powerfully into our life. Feathers and birds are associated with the element of air. Mental energy is given expression through speech, which also involves air. What we now do is breathe and speak our wishes into a feather and the bird energy will carry it forth to manifest it for us.

1. Choose a feather
It can be any feather. One from your own backyard is especially effective because these birds have a relationship with you and have chosen to be a part of your life.

2. Find a quiet place outside where you will not be disturbed.
Hold the feather in both hands by the stem and close your eyes. Relax. The more relaxed you are the stronger the energy will flow.

3. Begin slow, rhythmic breathing.
Inhale for a count of four, hold for a count of four and exhale for a count of four. As you do focus on your wish. Visualize it in as much detail as possible. Then as you exhale slowly and softly onto the feather, see and feel that wish released from you into the feather to be fulfilled. Continue for 5-10 minutes.

4. Speak your wish as an affirmation in between each breath.
The affirmation should not be "I wish…" Rather it should be something along the line of "I thank you for my ideal job" or "I am rich on all levels". It is not unusual that a breeze will pick up as you perform numbers 3 & 4. It is a powerful confirmation of the wish energy being set in motion.

5. Place the feather to work for you.
This can be done in several ways. The Native Americans used prayer sticks, small sticks to which the feather is tied. It is then stuck into the ground and remained there until the wish was fulfilled. You can tie the feather by a piece of string to a tree limb. Each time the wind blows over the prayer stick feather or the feather tied to a tree, the energy you breathed into it is released and grows stronger. If the feather disappears, as it often will, it is an indication that the wish has reached its source and will begin to crystallize for you.

When you have done this, do not check the feather for 3-4 days. Keep in mind that the wish will manifest in the time, manner and means that is best for us. If you are constantly checking the wish feather, you will begin to have doubts and they will delay and/or prevent the wish from manifesting.

Two Secrets to

Secret #1 - The Law of Giving

"You must be willing to give in order to have your wishes granted."

When I am setting in motion a new project or working to manifest some hope, wish or dream, I will perform a variety of anonymous, fun acts of generosity and kindness. Before crystals became very popular and few people had them, I would take small crystal stones, place them in envelopes, pick names from the phone book and mail them. I would attach a note that would say something very simple, such as: "So that you can have a little more sparkle in your life ...A Friend."

If I am working on prosperity, I take some one dollar bills and place them in envelopes with an anonymous note, such as, "So that you will always know you will be blessed in life...A Friend." After I became published, I would often send copies of my books anonymously to people, sometimes gifting whole sets to spiritualist churches and metaphysical groups that were working to become established.

Many times I take small feathers, say a prayer and breathe blessings into them. I then place them in envelopes and mail them anonymously with a note: "This is a magic wish feather. For three nights hold it in your hands and make a wish. Then place it in your pillowcase before you go to sleep. After the three nights tie it with a loose thread to a tree so that it will float and dance in the wind. When the feather blows away on its own, your wish will soon be granted." (Craft store feathers are very good for this.)

I always love imagining what these people think when they received their gifts. I could see them surprised and wondering, " Who sent this? And why? And what does it all mean?" They would be talking about it to their friends and their family. It would add wonder and mystery to their lives for days and would add a great deal of energy in turn to my own wish making.

Heeding the Law of Giving is critical to having wishes granted. There are many things you can do to work with it. Perform some volunteer or charity work when you start your wish making. Help someone out without being asked. You do not have to commit to a great deal of time and effort, but do it willingly and joyfully, knowing that it is a way of helping others. And yes, you do help yourself in the same process. Do not do it though with a grumbling attitude: "I have to do this or my wish won't be fulfilled." If you do, it will not work for you and may even backfire. You will have been better off not making the wish at all.

Powerful Wish Making

Secret #2 - The Law of Receiving

"You must be willing to receive what you wish for and you must demonstrate that willingness to receive it."

The Law of Receiving goes into effect from the moment we start to manifest anything and it always shows itself within our life within 24 hours. It starts small and subtle, growing bigger and more obvious. From the moment you tie your wish feather outside to a prayer stick or to a tree this law kicks in. Within 24 hours the universe begins to send us little gifts. It's a bit like a test to see how truly willing we are to receive the wish we are making. These gifts will come in many forms. They can be compliments, invitations, and offers out of the blue, etc. They are little confirmations that things are starting.

We need to accept, to receive these little gifts, to start the stronger magnetic pull so that our real wish will come to fulfillment. Our wishes are often blocked when we do not realize that this is happening, and do not accept the little gifts. For example, someone may pay you a compliment about something you are wearing. What do you do? Do you accept it graciously, or do you reply with something like, "What? This old thing?"

Other people may offer to give you something. What do you do? Do you say, "Oh no, I really could not take it"? Or what if someone offers to help you with something, what will you say? Is it something like, "No, thanks, I can handle it myself"? Or what if you get an invitation or two. Will you accept it or decline? Will you be just too busy?

If we do not accept the little things, the universe will not send us the bigger things. The wish we want to have fulfilled will not come about. By accepting the little gifts, we start a magnetic pull to us that helps manifest our hope, wish or dream.

When you release your feather outside to work for you, pay close attention to invitations, gifts and such that come your way. Accept as many of them as you can. And do not feel guilty about it. Guilt will block or hinder the fulfillment of your hope, wish or dream. It's a way of saying that you do not deserve to have your wishes fulfilled, and it will stop.

There will be a time in which you can give back, so enjoy the receiving! Think of it like Christmas or a birthday, a time in which people give you gifts because it is a special day. Our wish making is a special time, and if it is to succeed, we must treat it as such. Do you give back or refuse to accept your birthday or Christmas gifts?

Dreamcatchers and Protectors

Feathers have often been used to protect individuals while they sleep. Dreamcatchers are woven hoops with feathers attached. They are hung over the bed and they filter out the nightmares and negative energies that may flow by us when we sleep.

Simply hanging several feathers at the foot and at the head of the bed will do the same thing. Remember that contour feathers allow air to flow around the bird, facilitating flight. Feathers at both ends of the bed help dissipate the flow of negative energy and helps keep sleep peaceful and nightmare free.

Feathers can be worn on the body also to accomplish the same thing. Tying feathers in the hair, adorning a pocket with a feather or two or wearing feathers as earrings help dissipate negative energies. They are subtly fanned away. They are especially effective when we are in group situations and stressful environments.

Feather Cures for Aches and Pains

Birds often ruffle their feathers. Ruffling serves several functions. It helps to straighten out the feathers and it is also a stress release mechanism.

When I go into schools and teach about hawks, I usually arrive ½ hour early. This allows time to set up and it allows time for my hawks to relax from the car trip. Several behaviors inform me that they are relaxing. One of these is a ruffling and shuffling of their feathers over their entire body. The feathers raise up and the hawks shake. And the feathers and hawk settle down.

Feathers are wonderful for alleviating stress and pain. It is very good for headaches caused by nervous tension and for pinched nerves. Take the feather and softly sweep it along the part of the body that aches. Sweep the feather away from the body. This smooths the energy flow, eases tightness and alleviates the pain.

With aura dusting, described earlier, I mentioned keeping the feather 3-6 inches from the body. When easing aches and pains, you can touch the area of the body with the feather and then sweep it clear. (Do not touch the body with the feather of owl or one painted like an owl. Owl feathers push the energy deeper into the body.)

A mask of feathers will dissipate pain and sinus congestion very effectively. Place the mask on and ruffle the feathers. Breathe deeply and as you exhale softly ruffle the feathers with your fingers. Repeat 7-8 times and wait five minutes, The symptoms will usually ease within that time. Then repeat if necessary.

Skill
Development

Spirit Contact & Astral Travel

Benefits:

- **Increases awareness of spirit**
- **Facilitates dreams of spirits**
- **Improves sending and receiving spirit messages**

Traditionally there are two kinds of trance – mediumistic and shamanic. In mediumistic, the individual learns to withdraw consciousness from the physical body, allowing a spirit to communicate through it or overshadow the personality of the individual.

In shamanic trance, the individual learns to withdraw the consciousness from the body, leaving the body protected, and then goes out to communicate with the spirits directly, later consciously returning to the protected body. The soul, while outside of the body explores other dimensions, communicates first hand with spirits of various sorts and returns with full memory.

It requires much more development and skill for the second form. It is active, while mediumistic trance is passive. We live in a fast food society. People like their psychic stuff quick and easy and people do not apply the time and energy needed for shamanic journeys and spirit contact.

It is always more beneficial to develop and control our faculties than to simply sit, waiting to be used as an instrument. Consciously controlled spirit work involves taking our development directly in hand. Bird energy and feathers are wonderful aids to developing this ability.

1. Make preparations.
Make sure you will not be disturbed. You may wish to light a candle or use some unobtrusive incense. The incense should be light and airy, nothing

musky or heavy because we are dealing with birds. I have found flute music to be helpful.

2. You will need two feathers.
The feathers should be of the same species of bird. I often use flight feathers for this, but any type of feather will do, particularly if there will be astral journeys involved.

3. Hold a feather in each hand and begin to relax.
The more relaxed you are the better the exercise works. Allow your eyes to close and breathe deeply.

4. Imagine yourself growing lighter.
Imagine that with each breath the heaviness of the physical world begins to fade. Take your time with this. See and feel your aura extending out from you, expanding throughout the room, making your body density less. As you do, imagine the veils separating the physical from the spiritual becoming thinner and thinner.

5. Invite spirit to make itself known.
Mentally invite spirit guides and guardians to reveal themselves to you. Ask for the guidance and protection of the birds as you open to the spirit realm.

6. Pay attention to body sensations.
As you perform this exercise, the energy around you will change. It will require less effort. You will feel lighter. You may feel like your arms are helium filled and want to float. You may feel as if you are barely resting upon the chair. You may have the sensation of going over that dip in the road while riding in the car. You may begin to feel like you do in one of your flying dreams. There may even be an occasional jerking sensation, such as when you start to fall asleep and you feel as if you are about to fall out of bed.

7. Slowly open your eyes.
Spirit will let you know of their presence in subtle but very real ways. You may feel a soft brush of air. You may see shadows shift around you. There may be colored, flickering lights, you may see forms and shapes appear and fade. In the beginning it will probably be subtle things that you may wish to attribute to your imagination. Remember though that birds see and hear much better than we do. They can detect the subtlest things. Do not respond to them, simply note them and the sensations. Do this for only a few moments and then close the eyes.

8. Acknowledge the presence of spirit.
Even if you noticed nothing, acknowledge and thank the spirits for making themselves known. Courtesy is always most important. Ask them to give you confirmation of their presence in the next 72 hours. Wish them well.

9. Begin to return your focus to your normal world.
Breathe deeply, feeling your aura beginning to draw back closer around you. Feel yourself growing heavier and denser. Returning to your normal weight. Feel the chair solidly beneath you. See and feel the veils between the physical and the spiritual thickening and closing.

10. Perform a grounding.
This type of exercise can draw the consciousness away from the body and there is a need to ground. Slowly stretch, moving all parts of the body. Set the feathers down and feel your feet firmly upon the ground. Breathe deeply and open the eyes wide. It is a good thing to eat a little after this type of exercise. Nothing heavy but something to trigger the body's digestive processes. Digestion takes the most energy of any body process, and even if only digesting a few crackers it will ground us.

Initially do not repeat this exercise too often. Once or twice a week is sufficient. If you find yourself rushing home everyday to perform it, then you are getting out of balance and should cease it all for a while. Over the next few months you will find that it becomes easier and the confirmations become stronger. You will find that your dreams will become more lucid and astral projection / out of body experiences will occur. You will become more aware of the presence of spirit around you.

"Grandfather, Great Spirit, once more behold me on earth and lean to hear my feeble voice. You lived first and you are older than all need, older than all prayer. All things belong to you - the two-legged, the four-legged, the wings of the air and all green things that live.

You have set the powers of the four quarters of the earth to cross each other. You have made me cross the good road and the road of difficulties, and where they cross the place is holy. Day in, day out, forevermore, you are the life of things."

- Black Elk

The Dragon Shield

The dragon is a multi-faceted creature with a complex power and medicine. Though Christianity and the western world has made it out to be an evil reflection of the devil, it is the epitome of great pimal power. In the East the dragon is revered and honored. It embodies the forces of wisdom, strength, spiritual power and and the power of creation. It controls the climate - both of the weather and of our lives. To the Chinese dragons are the ultimate power. They can be as tiny as a silkworm or grow to fill the space between earth and the heavens at will.

When I teach workshops on magickal dance, a variation of an ancient dragon dance is performed and, usually within 3 hours (if not sooner) there is a change in the weather. If it's been sunny, it clouds up and rains or snows. If it is raining or snowing, it will clear up. Dragon energy is protective, powerful and life changing. Recently I used my dragon dance for a unique purpose.

I had returned from a trip into town. As I carried groceries into the house, about two dozen hornets swarmed around me. I discovered that they had built a nest next to the stairway. I knew they would have to go or we wouldn't be able to go in and out of the house without being attacked. They weren't willing to move, although there were acres of land they could use for their home. And they obviously weren't going to heed my"you don't bother me and I won't bother you" policy. The last time I tried to remove a hornet nest to the woods, I was unsuccessful and got stung a lot.

I performed my dragon dance and ritual, calling upon the dragon spirit to protect me when I cleaned them out. I asked for the smoke of the dragon to calm them and the wings of the dragon to fan them away from me and shield me if they swarmed, which was likely. I drew my dragon designs on my hands. My focus was on going to battle and being shielded because this is how hornets behave.

As I approached the nest, two of them were serving as lookouts, common among hornets. One buzzed around me and the other returned to the nest. I'm sure it was to call forth the troops. Surprisingly, only a few flew out of the nest, but they didn't come within two feet of me. The dragon shield medicine was working. In less than five minutes the nest was removed - quietly, quickly and powerfully.

Chapter 6

Medicine Shields

Shields have an ancient history. Their creation, decoration and application are varied, but in most societies the shield was as much practical as it was symbolic and sacred. Most people are familiar with the European shields, the Coat of Arms, and the medicine shields of the Native Americans. Both served multiple functions, as did the decorated shields in most societies. Their primary function though was for protection.

In Europe, heraldry became more formalized, but its origins and significance is just as symbolic as in those societies in which the methods were less formal. In most societies, heraldry (the creation and decorating of shields) was associated with armorial bearing and, originally, it served a practical purpose. Painting the shields helped identify opponents in battle. Since shields had a simple flat space, it was most practical for painting.

Many believe that the European heralds were originally minstrels familiar with the various coats of arms and who bore them. They came to serve an exaggerated function during tournaments and jousts. During these medieval times heraldry would develop its own descriptive language and rules. In other parts of the world it would remain less formalized but just as significant. The medicine shield of the Native Americans epitomizes this.

A shield reflects the individual's medicine. Medicine was not just associated with healing. The medicine or power was protection in battle, success in hunts, guidance in dreams and visions and even protection in choosing a mate. As in heraldry, the medicine shields can be simple or intricate. They can represent family, tribe or the individual. Unlike the shields of Europe, the medicine shields are usually circular. They represent the never-ending cycle of life, death and rebirth - no beginning and no end. It

Traditional or Non-Traditional?

There often arises concern as to whether we should hold to only the traditional methods of making shields. And there is great benefit in doing so. Aside from keeping the ancient art of shield making alive, it does allow you to tap into the great thoughtform of energy associated with that tradition.

On the other hand, many traditional artists and craftsman will tell you that the ancient people would have used easier and more effective ways of doing so if they had the capability.

Most of us will not be able to hunt, tan and stretch our own hides nor forge our own metals for shields. We do though have material that we can use to make them in our own unique way.

When we do so, that is when the magic comes alive. Until we take what we have learned and find a new way of expressing it with our own creativity, the magic often lies dormant. It is our creativity and unique energies which bring the shields to life. It is what activates their energies and ties us directly to the archetypal energies reflected in them.

reflects the Medicine Wheel, the Sacred Loop - the symbol of all of life's cycles.

Animals, real and mythical, that were significant to the individual would often appear on both heraldic shield and medicine shields. These are totems, and the shield bearer established a relationship with them by becoming familiar with the animal's unique characteristics. The animal totem can also be a special spirit helper to the individual, providing protection. The picture of it on the shield becomes a way of invoking its energy.

Recurring dreams or visions can be represented on the shield. Colors reflecting specific qualities were used in their creation. An individual's special gifts or uniqueness can appear on a shield in a symbolic manner. Shields are ceremonial, religious, spiritual and armorial. There are shields for countries, counties, towns, cities and families. We can have shields for different aspects of our life, or a shield that encompasses them all.

There is no limit to the number or types of shields we can have. We can create a shield for protection or a shield for healing. We can create a spirit shield for our work with other realms and dimensions. We can create a personal shield reflecting all aspects of ourselves - spiritual and physical. For our purposes, we will focus primarily on the shield of protection, although its construction and the manner in which it works apply to all shields.

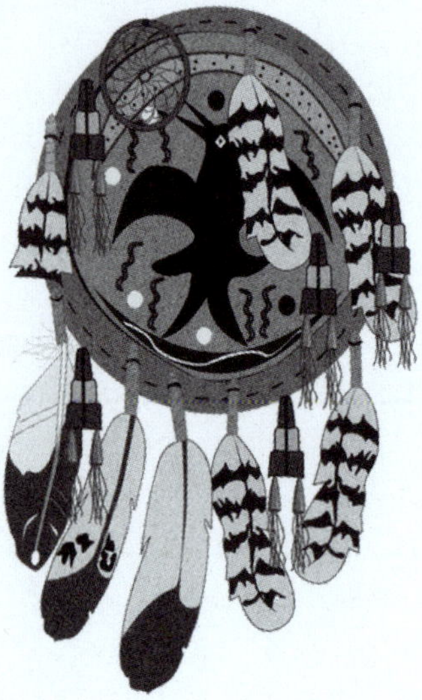

The Basics of

Although some societies had formalized rules for making shields, it is not necessary to follow such rigid formulas. Shields can be made from any material. They can be constructed from metal or upon cloth. They can be drawn upon paper or painted on a wall. They can be whatever shape we believe is most significant for its purpose.

Whatever kind of shield we make or however we construct them, there are three principles to keep in mind throughout the construction process:

1. **The creating and making of the shield activates your stronger creative life forces. This strengthens your aura and increases your vitality, starting the process of shielding yourself from outside forces.**

2. **The shield speaks of you and who you are.**

3. **All things made deliberately are accurate mirrors reflecting those who make them and the forces represented upon them.**

Whether we actually construct a shield or simply sketch or paint one, the process is powerful. On one level they become talismans, yantras and/ or mandalas. Mandalas and yantras are geometric designs created to express and invoke specific archetypal energies - in the physical or the spiritual realms. They awaken a sense of our relationship to us and to the forces of the universe represented on them. They provide bridges to archetypal forces. They link the physical and spiritual dimensions.

Shield Making

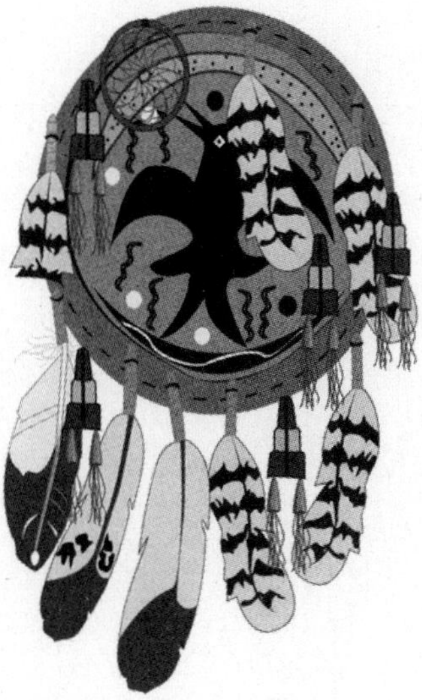

Mandalas hold the essence of a thought or a concept, and they are designed to draw our consciousness more fully into that concept. They stimulate our inner creative forces in a manner peculiar to its design. Shields, like mandalas, can be constructed to arouse any inner force we desire. It becomes a tool for integration and transformation. It becomes a tool of action and interaction with our life and us.

When we create your own sacred shield of protection, several things will automatically occur. We will find ourselves and our environment strengthened and protected. The shield becomes a mirror, reflecting its protective qualities into our life more dynamically. As the elements for the shield are brought together, balance and harmony begin to manifest during the construction process. While it is being made, aggravations begin to disappear and that which had not been working begins to work once more. Flow and balance begin to be restored.

The following are simple ideas that you can follow to create your own sacred shield of protection. Do not limit the creation to these ideas. Study heraldry. It will provide some wonderful inspiration. Follow your own heart in the design, using your creative energies. You will find that each one you create becomes more powerful and significant.

Common Heraldic

Heraldry is the creating and decorating of shields. They were used in battle and reflected one's clan and helped one to identify the enemy. The Coat of Arms now more often reflects ideals and symbols of belief.

TRADITIONAL HERALDIC VOCABULARY

BLAZON = the language used to describe shields of arms, crests & badges
DEXTER = the left side of the shield (as it is faced)
SINISTER = the right side of the shield (as it is faced)
FIELD = the surface of the shield
PER PALE = shield field that is divided vertically
PER FESS = shield field that is divided horizontally
PER BEND = shield field that is divided diagonally
PER CROSS = shield field divided into quarters
PER SALTIRE = shield field with multiple lines (diagonal)
ORDINARIE = principle shapes
CHARGES = significant animals, mythical beasts or inanimate objects; The animals were usually in one of four positions:

1. *rampant - standing on one hind leg*
2. *passant - walking past*
3. *displayed - outstretched wings*
4. *sejant - seated erect*

TRADITIONAL HERALDIC COLORS AND CHARGES

GULES = red (fire and fortitude)
OR = gold (purity and valor)
AZURE = blue (loyalty and truth)
ARGENT = white (peace and nobility)
VERT = green (strength and freshness)
PURPURE = purple (justice, majesty, royalty)
SABLE = black (repentance and royalty)
ERMINE = black tails on white (valor and leadership)
VAIR = pattern of blue and white (truth and purity)

Shield Symbols

CHARGES

ANCHOR	= *faith*	*APPLE*	= *good luck*
ARM	= *power*	*ARROW*	= *authority*
AXE	= *strength*	*BEAR*	= *defender*
BEE	= *industrious*	*BOAT*	= *venture*
BULL	= *protector*	*BOAR*	= *perseverance*
CRANE	= *vigilance*	*CROSS*	= *dedication*
CROWN	= *royalty*	*DOG*	= *fidelity*
DOVE	= *faith*	*EAGLE*	= *superiority*
HEART	= *gentleness*	*HORSE*	= *speed*
KEY	= *knowledge*	*KNIFE*	= *sacrifice*
LION	= *strength*	*MACE*	= *authority*
PELICAN	= *sacrifice and faith*	*SERPENT*	= *defiance*
STAG	= *purity*	*TOWER*	= *defense*
UNICORN	= *virtue*	*DRAGON*	= *knowledge & power*

Native American and

Different native peoples had their own correspondences in colors and animals. These were used in making the medicine shields. If you have ancestors linked to a particular tribe, you may find it more beneficial to study their correspondences. If you are drawn to a particular tradition, study it as well. Remember that the more significance you can realize, the greater the power your shield will have.

DIRECTIONS *(Seneca Tradition)*
EAST - *air; mind; creativity; yellow*
SOUTH - *fire; inspiration; purification; red*
WEST - *water; emotion; intuition; blue*
NORTH - *earth; body; prosperity; green*

DIRECTIONS *(Sioux Tradition)*
EAST - *wind; wolf; red hawk; red*
SOUTH - *fire; buffalo; bear; yellow*
WEST - *water; thunderbird; black horse; black*
NORTH - *earth; eagle; snowy owl; white*

DIRECTIONS *(Chippewa Tradition)*
EAST - *spring; eagle; red and gold*
SOUTH - *summer; coyote; green and yellow*
WEST - *autumn; grizzly bear; deep blues and black*
NORTH - *winter; white buffalo; white*

Shamanic Shields

Shamanic traditions in Africa and other parts of the word also used specific colors and animal images in making their shields. The animals imbued the shield carrier with its energy in hunts, battles and survival. Many shamanic traditions carved their shields from wood and then painted them with the various symbolic images.

African Style Shields

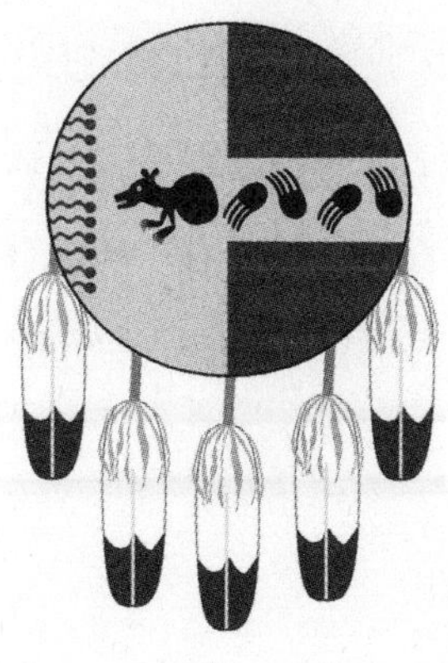

Tribal Shields

Prayer and medicine shields have been used in many traditions upon the planet. They are used to mark off sacred space, to protect, to heal and to help open to spiritual forces. We live in a time in which science has demonstrated that geometry affects electro-magnetic patterns - amplifying, diminishing, and even negating the frequencies of environments.

Shields can be created to induce altered states of consciousness, to stimulate peaceful sleep and to cleanse and purify environments. Some believe that they are merely a psychological sugar pill, a placebo, but we know that all energy follows thought. We also know that there is more going on with shields than a placebo effect, even if we don't understand it all at this time. Most of us do not understand how electricity works, but it doesn't stop us from using it for our benefit.

Skill
Development

Making Your Own Sacred Power Shield

Benefits:

- **Increases protection and healing**
- **Activates creative life force**
- **Strengthens and balances your energies**

Remember that the making of the shield itself is a sacred process, and the more thought and focus we put into it, the greater its power. Everything that we put on our shield will have significance. It is good to know why we use the colors you choose. Keep in mind also that the shield may change in the construction process. Although we may initially decide on a predominant color, once we get started, we may find that it doesn't quite suit us. ***HONOR THAT FEELING!***

Also remember that the creation of the shield is never truly completed. Over several months or even years, we may add new images, variations and colors to our shield. This simply reflects our growth and new depths that we are achieving. I have several shield designs that I created years ago that I am still adding to periodically. My totem animal shield has a multitude of animals on it, added to over the years. These animals include my power totems but also other animals that appeared in my life at significant times and for special purposes.

Additions to spiritual and protection shields are natural. They reflect changes in spiritual growth and perception. New symbols and variations will be added as our own spiritual depths expand. These changes are natural. Change is part of life and reflects an increasing variety of forces which are significant to us. These are forces that we have learned or are learning to draw upon and use within our day to day life.

Initially, we will want to draw or sketch our shield prior to actually constructing one if we choose to do so. Even the simple act of drawing it will actualize the energies associated with it. Anytime we do something physical like this, we are drawing those forces out of that vague ethereal realm and releasing them more dynamically within our physical life.

Concentration in the creating of the shield is important. Prior to actually starting, we may wish to meditate upon it, and once we start the construction, we must make sure we will be undisturbed while working upon it. Take as many precautions as necessary to avoid interruptions. The creation of the shield is an active meditation in itself. We are activating the right brain, programming it to respond to the images, symbols and significance of the shield and all of its reflective energies.

1. Begin by gathering together your materials.

You will need drawing utensils, paper, scissors, etc. If you cannot draw (or feel that you can't), obtain pictures of the protective animals that you can trace or cut out – if you are choosing to use animals. Do the same thing with any other protective symbols – be they animals, colors, geometric shapes or symbols of the various gods and goddesses to which you have an affinity.

If you intend to only draw the shield rather than actually make one, you will want to draw it eventually the size of poster board. This will make it easier to hang and focus upon in meditation.

2. Determine the colors.

Choose colors that are your favorite or that you find calming and protective to yourself. You may even want to use opposite colors as they balance each other: red and green, black and white, orange and blue, purple and gold, etc. When you choose the colors, learn something about their hidden significance. Most colors are symbolic, and a study of them may reveal much about yourself and the energies you will be invoking.

3. Decide on a basic shape for your shield.

It may be a typical heraldic shape or it can be any other shape. Again, the more significance we attach to the shape, the greater the effect. Geometric shapes affect electro-magnetic patterns. They stimulate and elicit definable effects. If unsure, I suggest using a circular or square field for your shield. They are effective for every type of shield that you might wish to create.

The following are some examples and their significance:

circle = wholeness, complete, circle of life, calmness
square = balance, solidness, the four elements, stability
triangle = power, amplification, energizing, strengthening
diamond = creativity, activation, stimulating
crescent = feminine, creative intuition, emotional calm
cross = balances elements, harmonizes opposites
6-rayed star = healing, strengthening and protecting

4. Create the shield.

Take your drawing paper or your poster board, and draw the basic shield form (circle, square or whatever you have chosen) in the center. Leave enough space around the edges that you will be able to add images and other symbols. Some people like to place the animal totems inside the circle, while others like to do so outside. For some the inner placement symbolizes the animals' energies alive and active within them. For others, the outer placement reflects their guardianship and protection of the life environment. One is neither better than the other. Whichever you choose, know why you do so. It adds power to the creation process and to its ultimate effectiveness.

Place in this shield the colors and other symbols that are significant to your life and to the purpose of this shield. Since this one is for protection and balance, ask yourself, "What other symbols and images do I associate with balance, health and protection?" Arranging them upon the shield is a creative process. Place them in the manner that is best for you. Just make sure that you know the purpose and significance of each. Use the colors in the manner best for you as well. Place them in different sections that you feel is appropriate.

Place something personal to you upon the shield. It should be in a central position. This is something that represents you. In this way the energies activated by the shield will flow into your life and center around you appropriately.

5. Avoid being critical of it.

The idea is not to demonstrate artistic abilities or lack of them. You are using the shield to tap into archetypal energies and to draw them out and manifest them more dynamically. Early shamans and primitive peoples are not considered artistically gifted, but their shields and drawings were imbued with significance and power that was very primal. As you imbue the making of the shield and all of its elements with significance, it will attain its own beauty and primal power.

6. Add to your shield from time to time.

If you reach a point where you are not sure what to add, just stop. You have probably created one that is suitable for you at the moment. Trust that it will evolve and change as you do. The shields will take on a life of their own as you construct or draw them. This is good! It's a positive sign that it is already working. You will also find in the process that you lose track of time. This is also a positive sign that you have touched and activated those archetypal energies associated with the symbols of the shield. You have been drawn into its energy.

Cottonmouth

We live in an area where cottonmouths are common. Most snakes will try to avoid contact with humans unless surprised and disturbed. A rattlesnake will even move out of the way most of the time. Cottonmouths do not. The cottonmouth is large, thick and aggressive, even moreso than what most water snakes are.

There are two small ponds on our farm. We are slowly clearing and converting the area to one that is quite magical. We were standing near the pond and my wife walked down to the edge in the grasses, looking for turtles and small fish. There was a rippling of water and a thick, three foot long cottonmouth swam across the pond away from her. She was standing right next to him. Knowing how aggressive this snake can be, we thanked him for responding the way he did. We told the cottonmouths that we would not bother them if they would not bother us.

Meditations seemed to reflect that a cooperative attitude was established with the cottonmouth. (But just in case, we began wearing heavier boots and carrying our staffs when we visited the pond.) My wife's staff is a snake staff. It has a vine wrapped around it, that looks like a thick snake. One of mine is dedicated to the dragon, relative to the snake/serpent.

Some time later I was clearing out growth around the edge of the smaller pond. I had my staff with me and had checked the grasses first for any snake. I stuck my staff in the soft sand at the water's edge and I began pulling out the weeds that were beginning to choke the pond. I had been working for several minutes, and as I pulled another bunch of weeds at the water's edge, there was a sudden movement and a ripple of water. I jumped back startled. A very large cottonmouth swam slowly away from where I had just pulled the weeds. I pulled them from around him. As I watched it swim off, its tail brushed my staff at the water's edge.

That he didn't strike was amazing. It was contrary to its natural behavior but it confirmed the sanctity of our agreement. The respect was there. And I have no doubt that it brushed my staff to let me know this.

Chapter 7

The Journey Staff

Wouldn't it be great to have a magic wand? We could just wave it around and our problems would disappear. If we needed something, we could shake it about and it would appear out of nowhere. Or how about a staff that could direct and focus thoughts and energies so that we could heal, bless and manifest things more effectively. Magical staffs and wands have come in many sizes, shapes and models throughout the ages. Mystics and shamans used a simple staff. Some Wiccans use the branch of a willow tree. Magicians of the past have used swords, athames and even a finger on their hand. Sorcerers and medicine people have used feathers and bones. Modern psychics make quartz crystal wands or attach crystals to walking staffs to redirect and focus energy.

What we often do not realize is that the wand or magical staff is just a tool. It is not the source of the magical energy but it does help focus and direct it. It can be used like an antenna. It can be a storehouse of energy that we can draw upon when needed. It is a source of protection. It can open veils help us walk between worlds and dimensions with greater balance. It can help us project thoughts and energies to heal and bless, to balance and strengthen.

All staffs are links to the ancient power, energy and spirits of trees. They act in many ways like a satellite of the tree essence and in order to understand how it works we must first understand some of the power and significance of the tree.

The tree is an ancient symbol. It has great spirit and it represents things that grow. It represents fertility and life. To some, it is the world axis, and to others it is the world itself. Its roots are within the earth, and yet it reaches to the sky. It is a bridge between the heavens and the earth, the mediator between both worlds. Through shamanic work we strive to bridge

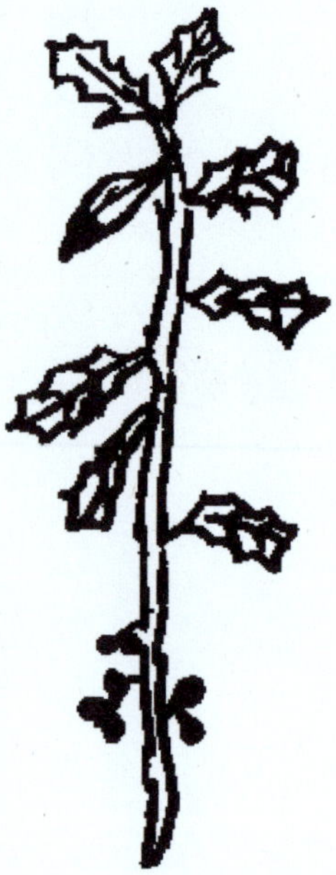

Holly Prayer Sticks

Holly is powerful to use for wands, staffs and prayer sticks. It is magical and can successfully be used by anyone with little effort. It is one of my favorite plants to use in magical wishes, for protection and for connection to the Faerie Realm.

Technically, holly is a bush, but it has all the power of a tree. Its essence manifests energy of protection. It has links to the archetypal energies of love, with an ability to overcome anger and hate. This is a plant whose energies can help the individual to awaken the Christ energies within, and can open one to angelic contact with time and effort.

Holly possesses the energy of the spiritual warrior, an energy that can be drawn upon in times of fighting and disruption. It activates the masculine energy of the individual in a creative manner. It is important for those who align with its energies not to scatter their own energies and activities. Any lack of direction may create problems.

This is a plant whose energies need to be honed and pruned and watched in order for the highest expression of it to manifest. Once done, it can stimulate a dynamic healing capability, one that can be expressed in many avenues.

Holly was sacred to the Druids. They kept it in their homes during the winter to provide a haven for the "little people." Carrying a holly wand or staff while walking in Nature at Dusk or dawn will open you to the phenomena of the Faerie Realm. The sounds and sights of this realm will begin to open to you more clearly.

one level of our consciousness with the next - one dimension with another - just as the tree bridges the heavens and the earth.

The tree, as the Tree of Knowledge, has been associated with both Paradise and Hell. In Greek mythology the golden fleece hung upon a tree. The Christian cross was originally a tree, and Buddha found enlightenment while sitting beneath one. Druids recognized the energies and spirits of trees, while the Norse honored Yggdrasil, the Tree of Life. Every civilization and traditions has its stories, myths and mystical legends of trees.

Trees bear fruit from which we gain nourishment. They provide shade and shelter. The wood is essential to the building of homes, and it is also essential to the making of paper - a source for communication and knowledge. The leaves of many trees fall in the autumn only to re-emerge again in the spring, reflecting the continual change and growth - the dying only to be reborn. We rake the leaves in the autumn, gathering what has dropped to create mulch for future plantings. Trees also serve as barriers, often used as a windbreak or fence by farmers. They are boundaries, whether separating one piece of land from another or one world from another.

Trees have always been imbued with certain magickal and spiritual attributes. The superstition of "knocking on wood" originated as practice to ensure no spirits were in a tree before it was cut down and thus inadvertently upsetting the spirits. In German folklore, the kobolde were spirits inhabiting trees. When these trees were cut, a piece of the tree was carved into a figure so that the spirit would always have a place to live. These carvings were shut up in wooden boxes and brought inside of the house. Only the owner was permitted to open it, and if anyone else did, the result would be untold damage. Children were warned not to go near them, and jack-in-the-boxes were fashioned to scare kids and remind them not to touch the real boxes.

Most people are familiar with the family tree. This tree has its roots in our ancestors, both familial and spiritual. All that we are lies in the roots of the tree, and thus all of our ancestry can be awakened through the tree. There are exercises that we can do with the tree of life to reveal ancestors and past lives that have helped create and nurture the tree we are now.

The tree has its roots within the earth and its branches extend to the heavens. Because of this it is both a wonderful symbol and a powerful tool for opening the energies of heaven and earth for us. They serve as a home and shelter for a wide variety of animals and thus they are a natural tool of the shaman. Ultimately, work with a staff will strengthen your focus, increase your abundance and develop your potentials. You will find yourself increasingly in a position of leadership and your role, as Steward of the Earth, will feel more natural. You will discover in time that your journey staff has become a tree from you fly or under which find shelter. You can follow its roots into the underworld and climb it to the heavens.

Choosing Your Staff

A journey staff can be used for many purposes. There are healing staffs, staffs for protection and even staffs to help open the world of spirit to us. I have a variety of staffs. One is a general all-purpose staff. One draws upon Dragon (and snake) energy for protection. One is for healing and I even have one that is based on my work with the Qabala. It represents the Middle Pillar of Balance. It is a work in progress as I continue to carve into it the various names of God and the angels associated with the Tree of Life.

Choosing and making our own journey staff awakens a powerful process in our lives. It is a commitment to the spiritual journey. It is the taking upon ourselves the path of initiation – especially into the mysteries of Nature.

Although traditionalists will tell you that you must cut down the tree that you intend to use for your staff, it is not something I recommend at all. There are dowel rods that can be purchased at hardware stores and at lumberyards that make effective staffs and wands. They can be decorated and painted with symbols that link to the energies of the tree. The second option I recommend is to find trees that have fallen and/or are lying dead already. Cut a branch or staff off of it. It is a powerful way of keeping the energy of the tree alive. (Even fallen trees still retain their energy until they have decomposed.)

If you must cut down a tree to use as a staff, then get permission from the tree and the landowner on which the tree is found. Taking it without permission is first of all illegal, and second of all, it is dishonoring to the tree. Sit and meditate. Ask the tree for permission. As a child my grandfather was often asked to find trees in the woods to transplant to the yards of friends and neighbors. He would walk through the woods, stopping occasionally, touching and even softly talking to the trees, until he found the one that was OK to transplant. When my brothers and I would ask, "How about this one?" He would usually shake his head and continue on until he found the right one.

If you must take a live tree, then plant a live tree of the same kind in its place. It is a way of honoring the tree. And do not take trees that are endangered, and I have found it beneficial to use trees that have several purposes, so that it is unnecessary to take endangered trees.

The kind of tree is individual. Each tree has its own energies and distinct properties. The list on the following pages can assist you in your choice.

Dictionary of Trees

Alder

The alder tree is one whose energies provide protection. It can awaken prophecy and has strong ties to the element of water and its force within the universe. The raven is an animal totem often associated with it, and the raven is a bird of great mysticism and magic. A staff made from alder can awaken the ability to open perceptions to the dark void. It has ties in mythology to the Celtic pantheon and the blessed giant Bran. It is a good tree to align with in order to overcome unawareness.

Apple

The apple tree has many magical, healing characteristics associated with it. It is commonly used for wands and staffs. It is sometimes associated with the Tree of Knowledge. The apple was considered the "Fruit of Avalon" that could endow the individual with magical abilities. Painting or carving the apple on the staff helps awaken the magic. The apple tree is also the home of the mythical unicorn. Its energies are such that it can stimulate healing on all levels. It bears a fruit, and its blossoms are powerfully fragrant and can promote happiness and success. Its energies are cleansing to the astral body. It activates the need to make choices within one's life, and to see that there are always options. In Teutonic mythology, the apple stimulates youthfulness and beauty. It also has ties to Aphrodite, as it grew in Hesperides.

Ash

The ash is the sacred tree upon which Odin sacrificed himself that he may achieve higher wisdom. The Teutonic gods held council under it each day. It has an energy that when aligned to will awaken greater strength and might. It is a universal source of light and life energy, amplifying the innate abilities of the individual. Using this as a staff will manifest opportunities to link the inner and the outer worlds. There were nine worlds in Teutonic myth, all located throughout the great Tree of Life. The energy of this tree can open us to the perception of how events and people are linked together. Its energy promotes learning to be at one with the self, without cutting the self off from the rest of the world. It awakens the development of sensitivity to great and small influences. It also has ties to Celtic mythology and the one known as Gwydion.

Aspen

The aspen is a tree whose name and essence brings upon the facing of fears and doubts. It is associated with the Egyptian symbol of the uraeus. It is a tree of resurrection, and can bring a calming of anxieties around changes within one's life. It releases energy into the individual's life that facilitates entering the subtler planes of life and greater soul fearlessness. It can open one to greater control of the dream realms of sleep. It can bring fears to the surface so that they can be met. Once met with determination, there occurs rebirth and the ability to overcome impossible odds. It stimulates communication with the higher self. This tree works well with snake medicine.

Beech

The beech is a tree whose energy and essence can awaken old knowledge and new expressions of it. It awakens the soul quality of tolerance, and its name and essence help align the individual with the higher self. It can be a staff that is beneficial for all patterns of growth. It can awaken greater opportunity to explore the past (immediate lifetime or past incarnations) and to synthesize that knowledge into new expression. This is the tree of the discovery of lost wisdom, and thus the individual must learn not to discount the knowledge and teachings of the past. It helps soften an over-criticalness due to the individual's past and balances oversensitivity.

Birch

The birch tree is one whose essence has ties to ancient forms of shamanism. Shamans used staffs of birch to awaken an energy that would enable them to pass from one plane of life to another. It balanced the shamans as they made such treks. Balance in the awakening of energy is the essence of this tree. It awakens the energy of new beginnings and a cleansing of the past. It manifests opportunities to clear out old ideas, those, which are no longer beneficial, as new energy must be purposeful. It is one of those energy expressions of nature whose name was renewed each year in varying ceremonies. Those who take upon this tree as a staff, must also learn to renew it and rededicate it each year. This is best done in the month of November, as November was the start of the Celtic New Year. Birch is known as the "Lady of the Woods," and it helps connect the individual to all goddesses of the woodlands. One is never to take its bark or a limb to use as a staff without permission of the goddess.

Cedar

Cedar is a tree whose essence will strengthen and enhance any inner potentials of the individual. Its staff has the energy of protection, and it can open opportunities to heal imbalances of an emotional or astral nature. This is a tree tied to strong healing energies. Cedar is a tree whose energies work to cleanse the auric field, especially at night while the individual sleeps. It helps the individual to balance the emotional and mental bodies and can stimulate dream activity, which brings inspiration and calm. It is a tree of consecration and dedication, and it has ties to Wotan. Tradition tells us also that the unicorn keeps its treasures in boxes made of cedar.

Cherry

The cherry tree is the tree of the phoenix, which rose from the ashes. One who aligns with its essence with a staff will find the energy and ability to rise from the fires of their own life in a magnificent manner. It awakens openness in consciousness and assists in the realization of insights. This is a tree whose essence can bring the individual to the threshold of a new awakening. It is up to the individual though to cross that threshold.

Cypress

The cypress tree staff awakens the understanding of sacrifice within one's life. It opens one to a greater awareness that sacrifice must not always involve pain and suffering, especially when the sacrifice is made for something or someone we love. Its essence can awaken the primal feminine energies, which reside within us all. It provides a manifestation for the opportunities of healing. It stimulates the understanding of crises, and it awakens the comfort of home and mother.

Elder

Elder literally translates as "old" and its energies are sacred to the followers of the old religion - especially those of Druid and Celtic tradition. This is a tree whose essence is that of birth and death, beginning and end. It is the tree of transition. A staff of elder helps awaken opportunity to cast out the old and renew the creativity of the new. It is a tree whose energy always manifests changes within the life of the individual, and change is beneficial, even if its benefits are not immediately recognized. This tree and its essence can help open the individual to a greater understanding of the ancient burial rites as forms of initiation.

The Elder staff links us to contact with the Mother Goddess in varying forms. It protects and heals. Its energies are dynamic and can be overwhelming at times. It is important to understand all the significance associated with this tree in order to balance the energies as they manifest within your life. It provides blessed protection and it brings magic to even the slightest wish. Magic with the elder must be controlled or it will manifest confusion and so working with an elder staff requires practice and care. It facilitates contact with the spirits of the woods, the Dryads, especially at the time of the Full Moon. It helps one to awaken a renaissance with the fairy kingdom. The elder tree is the mother who protects her groves and children.

Elm

Elm is a tree whose essence lends strength to the individual. It assists the individual in overcoming exhaustion - especially that which has accumulated over great lengths of time. It helps the individual to awaken to more universal sources of strength so that individual strength will not be tapped and expended. This is the Tree of Intuition. A staff from it assists the individual in "hearing the inner call." It is a tree strongly associated with the elfin kingdom, and alignment with this tree through a staff will assist you in attuning to those more ethereal beings of the nature realm. It is important though not to become lost within it or to become "fairy charmed."

Eucalyptus

Literally, the name of this tree means "wrapped, covered." Its oil was used in the Ancient Mystery Schools to wrap the aura in balancing vibrations, for they recognized that knowledge could bring an unbalanced awakening of the psychic energies. Its energies are highly protective and dynamically healing on all levels. Its influence penetrates both the physical and subtle energies of the individual, and it stimulates an opening of the brow chakra. Staffs of eucalyptus assist us in walking in the dream world. It can awaken the individual to full consciousness while in the dream state (lucid dreaming). It clarifies dreams and balances the emotions. It helps to bring out healing energies and an understanding of the causes of various illnesses.

Fig

The fig tree was the sacred tree of Buddha. Under it he found enlightenment. Its name and essence when aligned to awakens the intuitive insight that enables the individual to put his or her life into a new perspective. It releases past life blockages, bringing them out and into the open so those new thresholds may be crossed. It is a tree whose staff energies help the individual to link the conscious mind with the subconscious and to do so with the correct perspective.

Hawthorn

Hawthorn translates as "garden thorn." It is a tree symbolic of the energies of fertility and creativity. It is one whose essence will stimulate and manifest opportunities for growth on all levels within the individual's life. It is a tree sacred to the fairies. The hawthorn staff helps manifests opportunities for cleansing and the development of chastity that strengthens the individual's inherent energies and allows them to draw upon greater reserves. It provides protection against the inner magical realms, but the individual will have to learn not to act too hastily or the new doors will not be opened (and life may bring a thorn prick to remind you). It is a tree of magic - often of which those of the fairy realms hold knowledge. Once linked with properly, the individual's life will manifest many opportunities for new expressions of creativity and fertility. It is up to the individual though to act upon them in the appropriate manner.

Hazel

This is a very magical tree. It is a tree whose name is also a common name used in society by people. It comes from the "hazel nut tree" and indicates the quality of "quiet spirit." All fruit and nuts associated with trees are symbols of hidden wisdom, and this tree and its energies can bring out the opportunity to acquire and express hidden wisdom in a unique manner. Hazel twigs and even the staffs were often used as powerful dowsing instruments, being very sensitive to the electrical-magnetic fields of the earth and of individuals. Hazel tree staffs awaken the inner intuition and insight, and it is a powerful tree for stimulating artistic and poetic skills. It is often associated with "skaldcraft" of Teutonic lore. It awakens one to the true power of meditation, and it helps the individual develop a greater concentration of innate talents.

Heather

Heather is a tree whose energy can help the individual to awaken closer contact with the inner world of spirit. It can open one to the healing forces of nature and especially of the power for healing and magic with herbs. It helps the individual understand that healing begins within and not from without. This is a tree of fertility that can be expressed in many ways. The task of those who take this as a staff will be to learn to build upon a strong foundation. Looking for shortcuts or easy ways will create problems and demand correction of the past and the laying of a new and more solid-foundation. Heather represents immortality, and it facilitates seeing the immortal soul. For those undergoing an initiatory path, this staff will help to unfold the inner potentials. It brings beauty into one's life.

Honeysuckle

Although honeysuckle is actually a viney bush, it makes a powerful addition to any staff, when entwined around it. It helps us learn from the past (present life or past life) so that mistakes will not be repeated. It may manifest similar situations as have been experienced from the past, to enable the individual to deal with them more productively and to eliminate the karma of such. A staff with honeysuckle entwined on it stimulates a strong energy of change, and sharpens the intuition. It will open the psychic energies. It can bring revelations of hidden secrets, and assist the individual in developing sureness, while overcoming any tendency toward faltering. Opportunities to develop strong discriminatory abilities are awakened- especially in distinguishing the true from the false. The honeysuckle staff helps the individual to follow his or her own beliefs safely. It awakens versatility and confidence. The fragrance of its blossoms is "attracting" to those of the opposite sex. It also helps balance the hemispheres of the brain for more powerful expressions of creativity. It increases understanding of non-physical realities and has ties to the Celtic goddess Cerridwen.

Lemon

Lemon is a tree whose energies balance the aura and help to keep it cleansed of negative emotional and astral influences. This staff is especially important for those who are just beginning to develop and unfold their psychic energies. It draws protective spiritual guides and teachers into one's life, and it is especially powerful for anyone who does work at the time of the Full Moon. It brings clarity of thought. Its essence makes one more sensitive to using color therapy-in any of its forms. It stimulates love and friendship and it is strengthening to the entire meridian system of the body.

Lilac

Lilac is actually a bush but its essence activates a play of archetypal energy within our life that helps to spiritualize the intellect. It will align and balance all of the chakra centers of the body, and it draws protective spirits into our life. Although it is difficult to find a lilac large enough for a staff, it makes a powerful prayer stick and wand. They are decorated to reflect the chakras of the body in some way are powerfully healing. Lilac awakens mental clarity, and for one wishing to activate the kundalini in a balanced manner, it is excellent to work with like a staff. It has a strong tie to the nature spirits as they use its vibrations to raise their own consciousness. Various orders of fairies have always been associated with this tree. It can open one to a recall of past lives and can help awaken clairvoyance. Most importantly it manifests the energy that helps the individual realize that beauty is sufficient only to itself, and that there is a beauty inherent within all things.

Magnolia

Magnolia is a tree whose energies help to strengthen and activate the heart chakra, the center of idealism, love and healing. More importantly, its staff helps to align the heart of the individual with his or her higher intellect. It is a tree whose essence strengthens fidelity and provides opportunities for developing strong relationships. It is an aid in the opening of psychic energies, and can enable the individual to use that intuition to locate lost items, lost thoughts and lost ideas and apply them anew.

Maple

Maple is a tree, which helps the individual to bring a balance to the male and female energies within. It balances the yin and yang, the electrical and the magnetic. This tree's staff and the archetypal energies behind it help the individual to ground psychic and spiritual energies and to find practical means of expressing them within their lives. It is activating to the chakras in the arches of the feet, which enable the individual to stay tied to the energies of Mother Earth. For men, this staff is often beneficial to work with as it facilitates the awakening and proper expression of the feminine aspects of nurturing, intuition and creativity. The flowering maple has the energies of sweet promises and aspirations. It awakens the inner fire, which illumines without burning.

Oak

The oak tree was sacred to the Celts and Druids, and in the Teutonic mythology it was associated with the energies of Thor. It is a powerful symbol of the male energy, the yang or electrical aspect of the universe or individual. It is also aligned with all solar aspects of the universe. When a staff of oak is worked with, its energy awakens great strength and endurance - even through the most trying circumstances. It helps to manifest a stronger and more active sense of helpfulness towards others, and it opens one to more easily be helped by others. It is a tree with strong ties to the realm of nature spirits as well. The oak tree staff provides the energies to open the doorway to the inner realms and their mysteries. It awakens greater strength and security in all pursuits. It is a tree aligned with primal male force, which must be controlled and expressed properly. The acorn of the oak is a symbol of fertility and fruition and the manifestation of creativity. Carving or painting it on your staff helps awaken this energy. It represents the continuity of life.

Mistletoe grows parasitically upon the oak tree. It was sacred to the Druids and it is a symbol of the feminine energy. It is a reminder of the need for some expression of the feminine in all we do. It helps us link with all lunar aspects within the universe. It manifests energy of protection, particularly toward children or to the child within that the individual is trying to re-manifest. It opens us to recognizing the power and rhythms of change reflected within the lunar cycles, and it also increases dream activity. It has the capability of opening one to the primal feminine energies of the universe, but it may require sacrifice with joy in order to achieve such an alignment of such great intensity. It can be used to develop an "invisibility" or going unnoticed when desired, along with the ability to shapeshift. The mistletoe was a powerful herb of the Druids, used for fertility and as an aphrodisiac. It was a symbol of rebirth and the awakening of vision that could open the secrets of life beyond the physical. Its energy awakens the vision of one's soul life in the future. It can be attached to your staff with ribbon or thread. Some people take the mistletoe from Christmas each year to replace the mistletoe on their staff.

Olive

The olive tree is the Tree of Peace. It is tied to the archetypal energies of harmony and peace of mind, and when an olive staff is worked with, its essence will manifest greater inner strength and faith as true forces-not just as beliefs. It brings renewal and rejuvenation - restoring a zest for life. It is also linked to regeneration-in physical healing and in spiritual unfoldment. It enables the individual to access the levels of consciousness that manifest inner guidance and deep levels of clairaudience. It increases sensitivity, and renews the individual's hope and will to enjoy life. It is also known as the Tree of Honor, and it has ties to Athena, Poseidon and Zeus.

Orange

The orange tree powerfully affects the astral body and energies of the individual. Aligning with this tree through a staff manifests an energy that assists development of conscious astral projection, the rising on the planes. It brings clarity to emotions and can assist in releasing emotional trauma gently. It brings calmness to highly charged states. Its energies aid in the development of counseling abilities, and it can stimulate dreams that provide clues to deep-seated fears or fears of unknown origins. It releases tensions within the subconscious, and it can be used to create intense thoughtforms. It activates the spleen chakra, and it can put a person in the mood for marriage. The color of orange should be used in designs on this staff.

Palm

The palm is a Tree of Peace. It has a powerfully calming energy associated with it, so much so that it can provide protection for all members of a group tied to the one who has aligned with its energies. It makes a wonderful staff for groups. It manifests opportunities to celebrate or to produce something worth celebrating. The leaves alone have been rumored to prevent evil from entering into an area. It is an easy plant to grow indoors, providing a protective energy for the home environment. It can open one in meditation to a realization of the divine within, and it can ultimately help one to learn to commune with members of the angelic hierarchy. It awakens one to the Christ within.

Peach

The peach tree is tied to awakening hidden wisdom, as with all fruit-bearing trees. In this case though, the archetypal energies behind it can help the individual to develop a new realization about immortality and how it can be attained. The peach tree staff can open us to magic associated with youth and the prevention of the aging process. It is tied to a renewed activation of the individual's life force, the kundalini. It stimulates artistic energies and the innovative applications of them within the bounds of the individual's life. It activates energy within the aura of the individual that is calming to the emotions—of us and of those the individual comes in contact with.

Pine

The pine tree was the Sacred Tree of Mithra. It also has ties to the Dionysian energies and mysteries. It is balancing to the emotions, and it awakens the divine spark, which resides within the heart chakra for true salvation as defined through occult and Gnostic Christianity. Pine comes from a word that translates as "pain," and it is its essence that helps the individual to alleviate such within his or her life on any level. Pine has an archetypal energy that helps one eliminate feelings of guilt and over-emotionalism so that decisions can be made from as clear a perspective as possible. The pine staff heightens the psychic sensitivity while balancing the emotions as well. It helps the individual to express his or her creative energies without feelings of guilt and without allowing others to overly influence or manipulate. The pine tree is cleansing and protective against all forms of negative magic, and it helps to repel evil. It was a tree sacred to Poseidon.

Redwood

The redwood tree is one of the largest and the oldest of the living trees upon the planet. They are direct descendants from the time of evolution known as Lemuria. Alignment with their essence can open one to understanding the evolutionary cycle of humanity. The redwood staff enables the individual to put his or her life into an entirely new perspective. Its essence awakens a clear insight into one's own personal vision of life and what must be done to follow through upon it. It stimulates great spiritual vision-especially of the etheric realms. It activates the brow and crown chakras, although if not properly balanced, it will manifest as unbalanced imagination and even superstition. It awakens within the aura a vitality that is simultaneously soothing and stimulating. It awakens extended growth periods that will touch strongly upon soul levels.

Rowan

The rowan staff activates a play of archetypal energies that manifests opportunities for us to develop control of the senses - physical and otherwise. It links us to a powerful force against intrusion by outside energies (including spells and enchantment). This also involves those energies encountered throughout the day. Because the aura is partly an electro-magnetic field, contact with others throughout the day results in an accumulation of energy "debris." One who has aligned with the energies of the rowan is less likely to be affected by these extraneous energies as it serves as a cleansing force. Its essence can also help open one to understand the significance and practical application of the Norse Runes. The rowan staff manifests an energy that will assist the individual in developing discrimination, especially in balancing common sense with superstition. This is the tree of protection and vision. Its energies invoke all goddesses and assist the individual in learning to call up magic spirits, guides and elementals. Its energies enhance the individual's creativity.

Spruce

Spruce comes from a Russian word meaning "fine, smart." As a link to the archetypal energies of nature, the spruce staff is powerfully effective in awakening realizations as to how best to detoxify one's system and to balance one's energies on all levels. It opens us to a clarification of disease causes - as applied to the individual. It awakens dream activity that gives greater focus, and it can be used to discern proper spheres of focus for others as well. It is an excellent tree staff to work with for any disorientation or lack of direction. It amplifies healing on all levels, and it is calming to the emotions. It is a gentle awakener of the dynamic feminine intuition, and it can assist the individual in developing lucid dreams that lead to conscious out-of-body experiences.

Sycamore

The sycamore was the sacred tree of the Egyptians. A sycamore staff can be used to draw the energies of Hathor into one's life and individual energy field. It is a tree whose name means "fig." As such, its energies when activated help prevent any atrophy of higher abilities the individual has brought into this lifetime. The staff can open communication between the conscious and subconscious minds. It strengthens the life force of the individual and opens the opportunities to receive "gifts" from the universe. These gifts may come in the form of assistance, compliments, etc. It is important to receive them graciously, for if we do not receive the "little" things, the universe will not bring us the "big" things. The sycamore staff awakens the feminine energies of intuition, beauty and nourishment. It can open one to the energies of love and nature and all their magnificent aspects.

Walnut

Walnut is a tree that can activate the energies of hidden wisdom within one's own life circumstances. Its staff awakens the ability to make transitions of all kinds. Its energies are often catalytic in the manner in which changes will manifest, but once allowed to play out, *all* of the changes will be of benefit. It activates a cleansing of the auric field so that the individual can see clearly what needs to be changed and how to institute it from the clearest perspective possible. The walnut essence awakens the energy of freedom of spirit within the individual, as if breaking free of the cocoon. The staff helps manifest opportunities to follow one's own unique path in life. Whether the individual follows through on such opportunities is a free will decision. Its staff though activates the energy for initiating and initiation. It opens knowledge of the esoteric aspects of death and rebirth and how to apply them constructively within one's own life. The key is to be true to one's self when aligning with these energies. Self-deception and delusion results in chaotic disruption instead of creative transition when this tree is aligned to. It holds the power of rebirth.

Willow

Willow is a magical and healing tree. Its name literally means "convolution," and there is a convolution of energies associated with it. It stimulates an energy of healing on many levels, especially though in the areas of herbology and aromatherapy. The willow staff will manifest opportunities to learn and explore these avenues. It awakens a flexibility of thought, and its energies, when properly worked with, will help the individual to realize the very intimate link between thoughts and external events. Willow is associated with an awakening of the feminine energies, of going into the darkness of the womb and activating greater expression of them. Its staff opens "night" vision, or vision of that which has always been hidden or obscured. It aligns us with the rhythms of the Moon, and it stimulates great dream activity. Individuals who work with this staff must learn to work with their dreams and learn to trust in their inner visions.

The willow tree is associated with the goddess Brigid of Celtic mythology, and its staff can help one invoke and align with her energies as well. It awakens flexibility and many avenues of exploration. It awakens powerful opportunities for communication, and it has ties to all deities of other worlds. It is also linked to Orpheus who brought to Greece the teachings of music and nature and magic. It has always been said to make magical wands and staffs.

Healing Staff and Bird Medicine

Many staffs are ideal for use in healing. I have found that they work especially well when working with bird medicine. The following are some general guidelines.

1. If there is a particular bird that you work with in healing, make sure that you have a feather on the staff that you've dedicated to that bird. (Remember that the feather need not be an actual feather of the bird but one decorated /dedicated to it.) You should also wear a feather, linked to the bird, when calling the bird's energy so it knows whom to come to.

2. Bird feathers used in healing should always be kept with sage when not in use. This keeps their energy clean and strong.

3. Do not allow others to touch the feathers you use for healing.

4. Have the individual sit or recline.

5. Place the staff upright so that you are always between it and the one being healed. It is your antenna and directs energy to and through you. No other person should come between you and the staff. If you move to the opposite side, take the staff along and place it again.

6. Smudge the individual using sweeping motions with your aura duster. As you do imagine and feel healing air brushing in and around you and the person being healed. Imagine great wings of the bird surrounding you and the person being healed. Feel and see their energy being balanced and smoothed out. Work from the top of the head to the feet, clearing all energy around the person.

7. If you are working with owl energy, do not touch the person with the feathers, as it will push the imbalance deeper rather than drawing it out.

8. Then perform any other healing technique that you are inspired to do. Some find it effective to hold the staff over and around the individual, projecting energy directly from it.

9. Offer a prayer of thanks to the bird spirit for the healing.

10. Set the staff aside. Remove the feathers from it and yourself. Set them aside, protected and perform some grounding exercise.

Skill
Development

Making Your Sacred Journey Staff

Benefits:

- **Attunement to the spirit & energy of trees**
- **Activates creative energies within you**
- **Strengthens ability to focus and direct thoughts & energy**

Trees are patient. You cannot force the expression of their energy through your staff. When you plant a seed – which is what we are doing when we make our own journey staff – that seed needs time to germinate, take root and then work its way up through the soil. Do not assume that nothing is happening if there is no immediate noticeable manifestation of energy through your staff. If we wish to truly bridge to being a Steward of the Earth, we must persist. Everything that we try to grow within our life whether successful or not – adds to our innate power and wisdom.

1. Gather the materials for your staff.
Choose a tree or a piece of wood of a length that suits you. Reflect on its significance and on what you wish it to do.

2. Decorate your staff.
Use paint of colors that amplify and reflect the energies you wish. You may wish to attach feathers to the staff. They are particularly empowering to the energies, as the tree is the natural habitat for birds. You can also carve or paint the images of animals on it. If using a dowel rod to create the staff, you can use a wood stain appropriate to the tree whose energies you wish to invoke. You may wish to attach crystals of specific types to enhance the energies of the staff. As you work and bring it to life, imagine and feel its

energies growing stronger. If the tree that you intend to work with is a fruit bearing tree, paint or carve the images of the fruit on it to strengthen the ties.

3. Charge the energy of the staff and do this in several ways:

- Stick it in the ground next to a tree whose energy you wish to activate through this staff.
- For protection staffs, I will set them outside during thunderstorms, charging them with the power of thunder and lightning.
- For staffs to serve as an antenna for your psychic abilities, set them outside beneath the full moon.
- Set your spirit staff outside during times of the years when there will be meteor showers to charge it with the power of the heavens.
- Take nature walks regularly with your staff.
- Have it nearby when you meditate and/or perform ritual.
- Do not let others handle your staff in the beginning. There may be some staffs that you never want to let others handle.

4. Offer a prayer and thanks for the energy of this staff.

One of the best ways of doing this is by planting a tree. (See the exercise at the end of this chapter.) You may also perform a giveaway in the Native American tradition. Hold the staff above your head and lift your face to the sky and offer the staff to the spirits of the heavens and earth to use it through you for their benefit.

Skill Development

Empowering Your Journey Staff

Benefits:

- **Increases power, fertility and potential of the staff**
- **Improves intuitive ability to see connections**
- **Develops power of sympathetic magic**

This exercise is a type of sympathetic magic, but it is much more. It has great symbolic significance and very powerful effects not only on our staff but within our life as well. For those who may doubt that what we do on one level affects us on others, this exercise will demonstrate the reality of this magical principle.

1. Choose a tree to plant.

The process of empowering our journey staff and all of its inherent energies begins with a simple and fully conscious planting of an actual tree. This can be a tree for the outdoors or one that can grow inside. It must be an actual tree though, and you must actually dig a hole, plant the tree and tend to it. It is even more powerful if you plant a tree of the same type as your staff, but it does not need to be so. We may find it easier to begin with the tree we have always felt closest to - our favorite. We could also go out into nature and meditate on which tree might be best. We should never choose a tree simply because we feel it may have more magical associations. Those associations may not hold true or be as effective for us.

2. Reflect on your goals - immediate and long range.

Then we can choose a tree that is more appropriate for our goals. We do not have to know all that this tree will reflect. That will unfold as it grows and we nurture it, but we should be somewhat aware of its significance and our goals. Do we want a fruit-bearing tree? Do we wish to bear a lot of fruit in our own life? If so, we must consider that most fruit trees have specific stages of growth, and only bear fruit seasonally. It doesn't mean there is no growth at the other times, but it may be less visible, less tangible.

3. Plant the tree where you will see it everyday.
This is a visible reminder that as it grows and blossoms so will our own inner tree and the power in our staff. ***What we do on one level affects us on all other levels.*** This planting can be indoors or outdoors. If the tree is planted indoors, at some point we may wish to transplant it to the outdoors so that it can grow free and uninhibited. At that time, we may wish to choose another tree for indoors. When we do transplant it successfully to the outdoors, we will find that the power in our staff will increase dramatically.

4. The care of the tree is a potent part of this process.
As we prune and water this tree, we should be aware that we are also pruning, strengthening, focusing and fertilizing the power of our journey staff. We are enabling its power to take stronger root so that we can extend ourselves to the heavens.

The tree that we plant can be a wonderful way of empowering all of the exercises within this workbook. Remember that trees are a powerful aspect of the natural world with links to all animals. Work with them will strengthen our connection to the animal world. Before and after each exercise, we can take a few minutes and give conscious attention to the tree. By taking a few minutes to reflect on the tree, what it represents and how much it has grown at the end of the exercise strengthens its overall effectiveness. It enhances our concentration and focus. Just as a tree planted on a hillside can prevent soil from eroding, this simple gesture prevents the energy awakened from eroding away or being dissipated.

At the end of any shamanic exercise, we can turn the soil around it or just place our hands within its dirt at its base. This is a way of grounding the energy we have accessed, and it helps to release it more tangibly and solidly within our physical life. Although it may seem silly to some or even mysterious to others, it is powerful and effective.

Inevitably there are some that will say, "I can't make anything grow. Every time I plant something, it dies!" The planting of the tree is a physical act to release change into our life. Death is always a companion to life, and it is change. It is part of the universal life cycle: life, death and rebirth. If we are unable to deal with this aspect, we will have trouble with all aspects of life – magical or otherwise.

Difficulty in planting a tree that will live may be an indicator that the time is not right to work the tree you have chosen. Are you choosing a tree based upon the shamanic magic that you desire but are not ready for? Are you tending to the tree properly? Shamanic and magical practices to be effective must be performed consistently and responsibly.

On the other hand, we must keep in mind that the tree is an outer reflection of an inner energy. If the tree dies, it does not foretell our own physical death. Most often it reflects that an aspect of us that is no longer vital has changed. Maybe the chosen tree was not the best to start with. Some people choose a tree because of its extensive shamanic associations, but many trees are difficult to grow. Maybe the death of the tree only reflects attempts to undertake too much too soon.

With all work with shamanism, we must start simply. We must allow our shamanic journey tree (inner and outer) to grow at the rate that is best for it and for us. One of the qualities of all good shamans and magicians is patience. All magic has its own unique rhythm for each of us. Forcing growth impairs judgment. Seeds need time to germinate, take root and then work their way up through the soil. Unfortunately, we live in a "fast food" society, and people wish to have their psychic, magical and spiritual development quick and easy. They wish to pull up to the drive-through window, get their psychic and magical abilities and then drive on.

With this exercise it is easy to assume that nothing is happening until we see the plant working its way out of the soil. Magical Believing teaches us that things will happen in the time, manner and means that is best for us if we allow it.

If your tree does die, give it back to the earth. Thank the universe for its presence within your life - if only for a short period. Then get another tree. And another, if necessary. If we wish to truly bridge and unfold our highest capabilities, we must persist. Everything we try and everything we grow within our life - successful or not - adds to our life experience and our magical, soul development.

The Owl Mask

I was completing my book Magickal Dance and I needed some photographs to use in it. I contacted my friend Quenda Healing Woman about the possibility of using a photo of her sacred owl mask in the book. Quenda is a powerful medicine woman who works with owl medicine. She said that she would meditate on it and let me know. She soon called, agreeing to it.

Within a few days of her call I had a dream where the mask was hovering before me. The feathers started falling out and became sparse. As the mask hovered, I heard the words, "The owl flies silent." When I awoke, I called Quenda and expressed concern over photographing the mask. We decided to wait before making any other decisions.

As the time grew closer to visit her and photograph the mask I had a second dream. In this dream the owl flew to me. It had no feathers, only skin. It looked like a bat with an owl's head. It hovered before me and I heard a crow cawing behind me. I turned and it cawed and cawed and then flew off. When I turned back around, the owl was gone.

I called Quenda the next morning and told her we should cancel the photo shoot. The crow was telling me loudly to pay attention. Quenda said that I was probably right but to still expect a third dream, as owl medicine works in threes.

Two days later I had the third dream. Again an owl flew toward me and hovered in front of me. It was beautiful with a full body of feathers. The wings began to grow and expand, encircling me. I turned around, amazed at what was happening. As I came back to the front, I was inside a tipi.. The flap of the tipi was fastened to the outside.. I reached out and unhooked it. I closed it, refastening it to the inside. As I stepped back I saw the head of an owl painted on the inside flap, facing into the tipi toward me.

I called Quenda the next morning. We both knew that the right decision had been made in not using the owl mask in the book.

Chapter 8

Spirit Masks & Shapeshifting

Of all the shamanic arts in lore and in practice, none capture the imagination more than the ancient art of shapeshifting. Shapeshifting is the ability to effect a change in oneself, in others or in the substance of the environment. This change can be physical or spiritual.

In more ancient times there were certain individuals with a capability of living between the physical and the spiritual. They could adapt themselves and change their energies according to their life circumstances. They could shape and mold the environment, creating whatever they desired and becoming whatever they dreamed. These were the shapeshifters. They lived the dreamtime while awake or asleep. There were no limits to where they could go or who they could be. These were the alchemists, shamans, magicians and wise ones of our myths, tales and legends.

Folktales and myths around the world reveal heroes and villains alike with this most fantastic ability, the ability to transform themselves or others according to need or desire. In Greek mythology, Circe changed Odysseus' men into swine. In a Nigerian tale Nana Miriam transforms herself to fight a giant hippo and save the village. In Eastern Europe, Rumplestiltskin transforms straw into gold. For most people, tales such as these are the stuff of fiction, but there is more to them than mere fictional entertainment. They reflect a hidden ability within every human being. They are the outer reminders that our own dreams hint of.

Shapeshifting has been called many things throughout the ages. It has been called transformation, metamorphosis and even transmogrification. It has also been aligned with alchemy and linked to the transforming or shapeshifting of lead into gold. Although many types of shapeshifting are

Animal Dances

One of the most powerful ways of connecting with your totem and bringing its energy alive within your life is by imitating the way it moves and postures. Most traditions around the world had dances that imitated the movement of animals. It was a way of honoring the animal. It was a way of aligning with its energy. It was a way of invoking its energy into one's life. Today the animal dancing has become ignored and yet it is still one of the most effective ways of developing a dynamic connection with the animal.

If you wish to align truly and deeply with an animal totem, study the way it moves. Imitate the way it walks and the gestures it makes. The human body a bio-chemical, electro-magnetic energy system. Every time there is a muscular contraction and electrical stimulus is elicited within the body. When we imitate how an animal moves we are changing our body's electrical system. We are making it similar or resonant to that of the animal.

For example, if we need to be more bearlike in a situation, let's move and posture like a bear. It aligns and creates resonance between our system and that of the bear. This makes it easier to express those bearlike qualities. This is the beginning of shapeshifting.

Most of the martial arts are based upon how animals defend themselves. Most yoga asanas are based on how animals move and breathe. We can use these traditions to help us begin this process. When we do something physical to align with and connect with the animal, we become empowered and the energy of the animal becomes stronger within our life.

The cobra posture of yoga is a powerful way of connecting in with snake energy.

described in literature, the most common kind is zoomorphism - the change from human to animal form. Of its many variations, aeluranthropy and lycanthropy are the two most familiar. Aeluranthropy is the human transformation into a cat. This was depicted in more recent times in the movie *CAT PEOPLE* starring Malcolm McDowell. Lycanthropy is the transformation of humans into wolves, and there are few who have not seen on screen or read in books tales of the wolfman. It is by no means confined only to these forms though.

Many of the stories and tales of physical transformation are merely symbolic, or they reflect a time in the evolution of humanity when we were not so solidly locked within the human form. In those earlier times, we may have been able to mold our shapes more easily. When the human body was less dense, we may have been able to metamorphose into other forms. It may still be possible, as all things are within the realm of possibility, but as yet it is beyond my scope of demonstrating. Over the years, I have heard of individuals capable of performing this kind of physical transformation, but I have never seen a legitimate demonstration of it.

Shapeshifting is Natural for Us

On the other hand, our auras (the energy field surrounding us) can be changed to take the form of an animal or creature. In such changes it becomes easier to express the qualities of the animal or creature. We can learn to move in and out of dreams in the forms of different animals, and many find it easier to initiate a conscious out-of-body experience in the form of an animal. We can perform ecstatic dances and rituals that create such a powerful change in consciousness that we feel as if we are actually changing and becoming the animal or creature. In such cases even though we may not physically change to observers, internally we may have a profound transformation, which can be accompanied by dramatic physical responses.

These inner transformations can stimulate tremendous healing, higher consciousness, out-of-body experiences, spiritual and creative illumination, heightened spirit contact - along with many other benefits. They should not be treated casually or lightly dismissed simply because no physical change is observed, for these activities ARE techniques of shapeshifting. They are in fact part of what you will learn to do through this text.

Shapeshifting is natural and instinctual within humans, but it also involves more than just transforming oneself into a beast. Everyday we shift our energies to meet daily trials, responsibilities and obligations more effectively. We learn early in life the use of camouflage, merely one tangent within the art of shapeshifting. We learn early in life when and how to smile to cover what we are feeling or to express open friendliness. We learn when to be serious and how to be apologetic. We learn how to seem studious. I know of no one who didn't learn how to appear innocently studying during his or her early years of school. All of us express a wide variety of personas according to need.

Our body language reflects much of our instinctual potentials for shapeshifting. We have all learned and practice behaviors and postures that make us more or less vulnerable. We fold our arms in front of us if intimidated. We look down or away if lying. Many of our behaviors and shiftings are so natural, that we do not even think of them consciously.

A shapeshifter is one who can relate to and adjust behaviors and energies to work and live more effectively as the conditions warrant - to facilitate drawing upon whatever qualities or energies are necessary. It is a matter of controlling and utilizing one's highest energies and potentials. It has both practical and mystical applications and benefits.

Applications of Shapeshifting

Practical

- Develops relating to people, work and life better
- Develops gentleness while capable of expressing great strength
- Develops self-discipline to achieve a goals
- Develops adaptability to any change that presents itself,
- Develops ability to turn foul moods into a pleasant ones
- Develops creative possibilities within limitations
- Develops putting aside hurt and/or fear to accomplish a tasks
- Develops skills to transform the pains & hindrances of life
- Develops stronger observation skills.

Mystical

- Strengthening the aura.
- Facilitating lucid dreaming.
- Invisibility.
- Healing.
- Spirit contact.
- Traveling within the spirit world & assisting out-of body experiences.
- Connecting to nature.
- Physical and psychic protection.
- Aligning with one's spirit animal/totem.
- Creating greater flexibility and adaptability to life - physical & spiritual.
- Creating inspiration and intuition.
- Traveling through time.

The Power of Masks

Masks have always seemed to have a magical power about them. Concealed behind it, we could become something or somebody else. We can become whatever we want to be by wearing a mask. Whether a simple headdress or helmet mask, it helped to enlarge you. To own a mask is to possess a potential power. The wearer magically assumes a new identity. It enables present reality to be suspended.

Masks are invested with mystery. They are tools for transformation. They are equivalent to the process of chrysalis. Metamorphosis usually is and should be hidden, so it is not interrupted. The hidden aspect, the secrecy, leads to transfiguration. It helps us to change what we are to what we want to be, giving us magic.

There is an ambiguity and an equivocation about masks. The ambiguity is the fact that when we wear one, we are no longer whom we thought. The equivocation is that we are making ourselves one with some other force. By wearing a mask, we become part of the mythical "'Tween Times and Places". We move into an intersection between the outer real world and other dimensions. We create a doorway of the mind and in the physical world - a threshold that we can cross to new dimensions and beingness. When working with animal masks, we move into a more intimate realm of animal connections. We are less passive and more active, bringing the energy of the animal alive more strongly within our life.

Mystery of Mask Making

The origin of masks is unclear, although there is very ancient evidence of their use all over the world. This evidence has been found in artifacts and in literature. The Tibetans wore masks to represent ghouls and skeletons in devil dances at the seasons of the year. The Chinese used papier-mache masks in religious drama. On Java, people used masks of wood in celebrations and ceremonies, often supplemented with shadow puppet presentations. The Suka males of the Congo during ceremonial dances following circumcision rituals wore helmet masks. The Aztecs used mosaic masks for worship and celebration.

The Greeks in their amphitheater wore large masks so the audience at a distance could see them. They were constructed with a tube to amplify the voice. The miracle and mystery plays of the early church often involved the priest wearing masks to represent metaphorical ideas such as death, the devil and life itself. In Italy full face, half-face and masks with beaks became an art form during the Renaissance. Mummers in Great Britain and in colonial

America were masked actors who around Christmas time portrayed characters such as Father Christmas.

To the North American native peoples spirits influence all aspects of life and are found in all things. To the Inuit of the Bering Sea even gnarled driftwood has an "Inua", a dwelling force that gives it meaning, real existence and life. Such pieces of wood were often carved into masks or made a part of a mask. Different Native American societies had their own mask making techniques and rituals. The Iroquois had their twisted facemasks. The Pueblo have their kachina masks, and the Inuit their wooden masks.

Native masks of North America often represented spirits that influence all of life. Rituals and masks were created to both appease and/or invoke. Masks were made of wood, fur, gourds and other materials. The Mandan made masks from the heads of dead animals

In Africa and America alike, most masks were considered the property of the secret societies, and only the members were allowed to wear them. When they were not in use, they were always kept covered. And no two masks were ever alike. Often men were only allowed to wear the masks, but women also had their secret societies, possessing their own masks. Every mask was individual, and each had its own story.

Masks have served a variety of purposes:

- Worn ceremonially to appease certain forces
- Worn to communicate with the spirits and the supernatural
- Worn to scare children and give them warnings
- Worn to terrorize the enemy
- Worn to represent mythological being or creature
- Worn to connect with animals or some other force in nature
- Work to make rain or control the elements
- Worn to prevent illness and cure disease
- Worn for drama and theater, storytelling
- Worn to facilitate shapeshifting
- Worn to court a lover, for fertility and sexuality
- Worn for amusement and ornamentation
- Worn as ornamentation, and for ritual and initiation
- Worn to represent family and clans

Ceremonial Masks

Traditionally masks were made to frighten away natural enemies, to resist evil spirits, for protection, for success and for fertility. In ritual, they can be used for almost any purpose. The masks can be worn or they can be used to decorate the temple area as well. Masks help us to enter into the imaginative world. They facilitate creating illusions. They facilitate connecting with the supernatural. They help suppress one's personality while encouraging the assumption of another. They are a dynamic tool for shapeshifting in they help bring out the persona and energy associated with it - be it a deity or a warrior.

There are many types of masks. There is the stick mask, which is difficult to employ in magickal dance. It doesn't leave both hands free. There is also the domino mask that was first used in 16th century Italy. These masks are the most popular. They cover the upper half of the face - some as far as the lips and some only as far as the nose. There are hat masks, which rest atop the head and generally leave the face uncovered. There are full helmet masks, which encompass the head and face, often resting on the shoulders.

Stick Mask

Domino Mask

Eagle Head Hat Mask

Twisted Face Helmet Mask

Iroquois Masks

The Iroquois nation is comprised of six major tribes: Mohawk, Oneida, Cyuga, Seneca, Onondaga and Tuscarora. All believed that evil spirits caused disease. At such times they would seek the assistance of someone from the False Face Society. An individual could only become a member of the False Face Society if he or she had been cured by the society. It was comprised mostly of men. The individual also had to have dreamed of it. In the dream, the dream spirit instructs the individual how to make a healing mask and gives the individual a healing song. Usually this dream had to be confirmed by another member of the society.

New members had to learn rituals and the songs of the society. They were required to create an elaborate costume to completely conceal the identity. The making of the mask was very ritualistic. A tree would be picked out, and the bark peeled from a section of it. Then a rough outline of the mask would be carved into the tree. The mask was then to be cut out of the tree without harming the tree. If the tree were chosen in the A.M., it would be predominantly a red color. If in the P.M., it would be predominantly black. Often the masks would have three colors.

Their masks were oval shaped with twisted and exaggerated features. The nose was large, protruding and often broken. The mouth was its most distinguishing feature, always taking an odd shape. The hair was made of yarn or vines, twisted and attached.

Making a Paper Bag False Face

1. Take a brown paper bag that will fit over your head.
2. Make sure the bottom of the bag rests on the shoulders and the top on the head.
3. Use excess at the open end to make a fringe:
4. Mark the eyes and cut out the eyes.
5. Choose three colors.
6. Make the eyes different sizes. The eye holes may be the same size, but you can paint around them to make them appear different sizes.
7. Give it a crooked nose.
8. Make the mouth twisted and very large.

Northwest Masks

The natives of the Northwest are of many tribes, but their masks were often similar in style. Their masks mixed fear, reverence and acceptance of spirits. They also were often totem related. Totem comes from the word "otoman" meaning "his brother and sister kin". In the Inuit traditions there were many clans. These clans are related through common ancestry. This ancestry could be human or divine, as gods and supernatural beings were often considered ancestors. The clan crest was often reflected within the totem poles, the masks and the fronts of the house.

Among the Inuit peoples was the belief that all things and all creatures possessed spirits. Every animal, object, element and place had its spirit. Every mask had its own story and dance to a particular spirit. Their masks were important and no two were alike. They were used for religious, social, healing, fun and ritual purposes. They even had their own secret societies. They also created transformational masks (one or more faces hidden behind an outer face. Unlike the Iroquois, among the Inuit the right to be a mask carver was most often inherited. Their masks were often imaginative, but they usually resembled humans, animals and/or birds.

Dancing and masks went hand in hand. Every mask had a story, a dance and a song. These were used in various activities. The Messenger's Feast was a masked ceremony in which hunters would seek favor from animals for food. The kazgi was a ceremonial house for festivals in which masks and dances formed a predominant part. Every family and clan had its shaman. This shaman was the healer and a spiritual leader.

The mask of the shamans had some common characteristics. They were always ugly faces. They also had a large tooth sticking out of the mouth. The mask was often splashed in red, dripping blood and they were made in the image of a guardian spirit that had been dreamt of.

The clan or totem mask reflected the protective energy of the guardian animal spirit. It was often carved out of wood or attached to a stick. The yes were the most distinguishing feature. The eye patterns were oval or round. Sometimes they were crescent shaped, teardrops or just slits, regardless of what the animal's natural eyeshape was. The masks were often left unpainted or only soft colors were used. If it was a spirit mask, it would be given a white face.

Kachina Masks

There were three main tribes among the Pueblo peoples: the Hopi, the Zuni and the Acoma. They communicated with the gods through spirits called kachinas. The Apache and the Navajo also had kachinas. Every kachina has a name, an appearance and its own unique power.

One legend tells how Kachinas taught the Pueblo how to hunt, fish, and make useful things. Eventually humans began to quarrel with them, so they left, going deep into the earth, leaving their masks behind. When the masks are worn, the kachina enters the individual and gives the person power. Each kachina had its own mask, dance and' ceremony. Each person had to make his/her own mask. The mask had to be in perfect shape to be worn in ceremony. Throughout the year, the masks are fed by sprinkling them with cornmeal and pollen to renew their powers. Navajo and Apache would simply wear their masks until they were worn out or the magic was gone.

Most of the Kachina masks were helmet types, often square or cylindrical in nature. Great care was taken in their construction. The choice of colors, the placement of colors, etc. - every aspect was symbolic. The colors were most often bright:

Yellow	-	north or northwest
Blue-green	-	west or southwest
Red	-	south or southeast
White	-	east or northeast
All together	-	zenith or sky
Black	-	nadir or below

Symbols are painted on the forehead and cheeks. This could be animal and bird tracks, clouds, lightning, sun, moon, stars, and vegetation symbols. Vertical lines under eyes indicated a warrior and phallic symbols were used for fertility.

Real eye openings are slits and have no relation to the visible eyes painted on the mask. Eyeholes are usually small circular holes or narrow slits. The painted eyes may be round, rectangular or half moons The nose is seldom realistic or seldom seen. It is often left out of the mask. The mouth is often painted in different shapes. Beaks, tubes and snouts are often used. They are often painted on in geometric shapes.

Kachina masks are almost always colorful. The shapes and features are often geometric and the left and right sides do not always match. Above all else, it should suggest a characteristic or force.

African Masks

The first masks were probably animal. Remnants of crocodile and elephant masks are as common in Africa as are the wolf and raven in America. Antelope and leopard masks were also common. Dances were constructed with them. The eland and the antelope were sacred to the Kalihari, and masks and dances were used to honor them. The antelope spirit taught the people how to dig the earth, and thus ritual dances were created with antelope masks to help seeds grow. The Oloko of Africa had masks to represent the leopard warrior. African masks though could also represent spirits or humans. The masks of West Africa are probably the most abundant and colorful. The Senufo people of the Ivory Coast have a rich tradition of masks, dance and music.

West Africa is rich in the variety of masks. They served many functions and often had multiple meanings. Often only the men were allowed to wear the masks, but there were secret societies of both men and women, each society possessing its own masks. Only members of those societies were allowed to wear the masks. The masks were kept in secret places, often hidden away in sacred woods. A juju house is a house where the masks were made and readied for ceremony. The windows were covered so that no one would be able to see inside and observe the sacred preparation and transformation.

Masks were used in initiation ceremonies, especially along the Guinea coast. In the Congo, masks represented demons and spirits. In some parts of Africa, masks were purely ornamental. The Bini of Southern Nigeria made ornamental masks of ivory.

Masks were most often used in conjunction with sacred dances and ceremonies. Drumming was a significant part of these rituals. Drumming and chanting was a means of calling to the spirit of the mask. The drumming and chanting often had a rhythm of three. The balafon is a wooden xylophone common to the Senufo people of the Ivory Coast and was often used in the ceremonies. The stilt dancers of the Dan people would incorporate bell ringing. Their standing upon stilts represented their ability to sit upon air. They would ring their bells and dance about chasing off witches and demons from the village.

Making and

Masks have been made from a variety of materials. These include, but are not limited to, fiber, wood, shell, bone, feathers, hides, cloth, bark, leaves and even husks. The materials and the making of the masks were done usually in solitude and with great deliberation and concentration on the force to be awakened by the mask. The mask making was never rushed.

1. Know what force you wish your mask to represent.
The more significance you can find in it, the greater ability it will have to help you make the transformations you wish.

2. Mask making does not need to be a complicated affair.
Begin with simple masks, so that you can experience the enjoyment of the creative process and be more free to feel the energies awakened by the mask. (The simplest masks are those made from paper. A plain paper bag provides many possibilities.)

3. Don't rush the process or compare it to others.
What you do with your mask will be most effective for you. Take your time, and keep in mind that with each part of the process - when done with deliberation - you empower the mask to help you begin to shapeshift to a new expression of energy.

4. Make your mask as comfortable as you can.
Remember that a mask needs airholes to enable you to breathe. Although some traditions have utilized a "bondage" or sensory- mask for specific initiation purposes, these were only employed under the strictest conditions because of their ability to augment radical changes in consciousness.

5. Be elaborate with your materials.
Subtlety has its place, but most masks have an exaggerated quality about them. It helps the individual to make the shift in consciousness to that which is greater than the self.

6. In most societies, the eyes were the most important part.
The eyes, as the window of the soul, have great play in mask making. In the different types of masks and their construction that we will work with later

Using Masks

on, be particular about the location and shape of the eyes. The eyes will convey the character of the mask.

7. **Use ordinary and simple materials in making your masks.**

Keep in mind though that as you do, you are using the ordinary for extraordinary purposes. It is a reminder that no matter how ordinary or inconsequential we may feel our life to be we can still manifest the extraordinary within it. Use beads, dried flowers, feathers, lace, paints, rhinestones, ribbons and whatever you have available. Be as elaborate with the materials as you wish.

8. **When you are not using your masks, keep them covered.**

It makes them more powerful, and the energies evoked by them are not allowed to leak or dissipate. It is a way of reverencing and honoring the forces of the mask. For temple masks, or those that are hung for decoration, this is not necessary. Temple masks are often reminders to us of the forces within our life. If you choose to make the wall mask more powerful for you, you may wish to have candles next to it. The lighting of the candles can be visualized as the igniting and activating of the forces represented by the mask.

9. **Use your imagination in the creation of the mask.**

Your designs and the forces you invoke through them are only limited by your own imagination. Masks help us make transitions from our ordinary levels of consciousness to those beyond. As you open and express your imagination through the creation of the masks, you expand the opportunities to connect with greater power and force. You move closer to the primal energy and essence that is you or part of you. Above all have fun with the process. Creation and imagination are necessary to enjoy ourselves fully.

10. **Use ritual to help awaken the power of the mask.**

Ritual dances are very effective for this. Later we will learn to use masks to create rituals for whatever purpose we desire. Ritual dances help make lifeless masks animated. Ordinary ceremonies become dynamic spiritual dramas. Masks and movement empower each other. The making of a mask is fun, but the mask to be effective must be secure and comfortable and it should not restrict breathing, speech or sight.

Skill Development

Making Raven and Owl Masks

Benefits:

- **Improves ability to connect with totems**
- **Improves intuitive and creative abilities**
- **Develops strong connections to raven and owl.**

To own a mask is to possess a potential power. The wearer of a mask can magically assume a new identity. Through it reality can be suspended. All ancient societies recognized this. It was most evident among Native Americans and in the shamanic societies of Africa and other countries. Mask making is an ancient craft. Many societies considered it an artform in many instances. Masks were made from a variety of materials - including feathers, stones, jewels and wood.

The basic principle of mask making is to know what force you wish to represent. Gather your materials. Use colors appropriate for your purpose and be creative in this process.

The Raven Mask

1. Take a large piece of paper or cardboard and fold it in half.

The paper must be large enough so that the vertical bar shown in the diagram will go over the top of the head. The horizontal bar must be long enough to go around the head and overlap in the back. When the horizontal and vertical flaps are fastened, the mask will fit over your head like a hat.

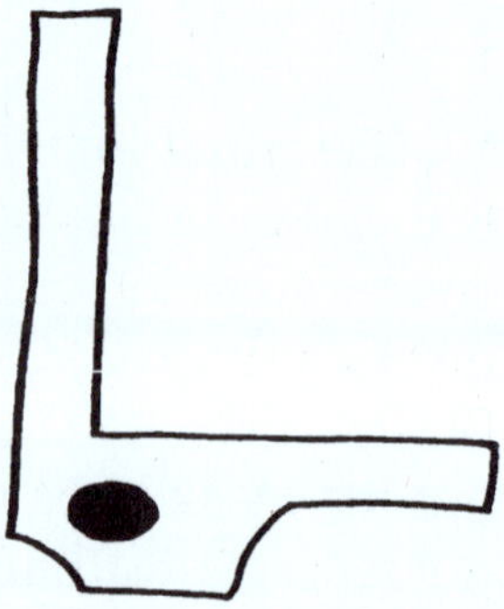

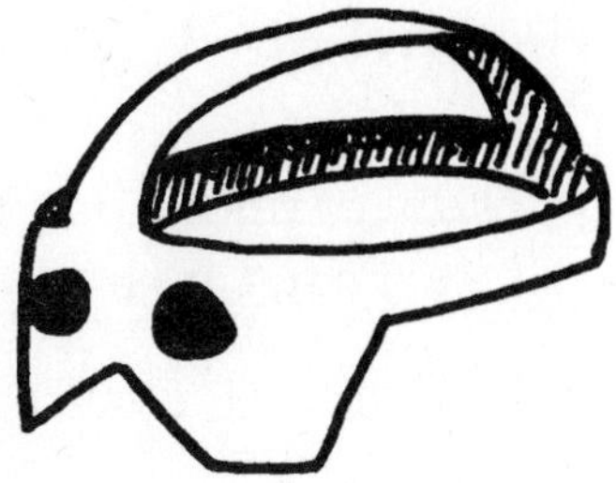

2. **Adjust the fit so the mask will rest comfortably on the bridge of the nose.**

The basic shape is the foundation upon which you can make a wide variety of mask images – animal and human.

3. **Take a second piece of paper and fold it in half.**

Sketch the pattern as shown in the illustration. The more curve you put in the bottom part of the drawing the more curve the beak will have.

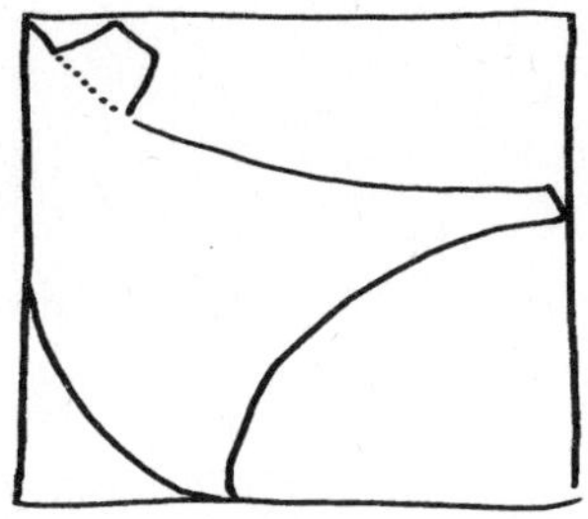

4. **Now cut along the lines and fasten it onto the basic shape described in step 3.**

The small flaps are fastened to the outside of the basic shape or you can cut two slits and feed them through. They can be glued or fastened on the inside and won't show.

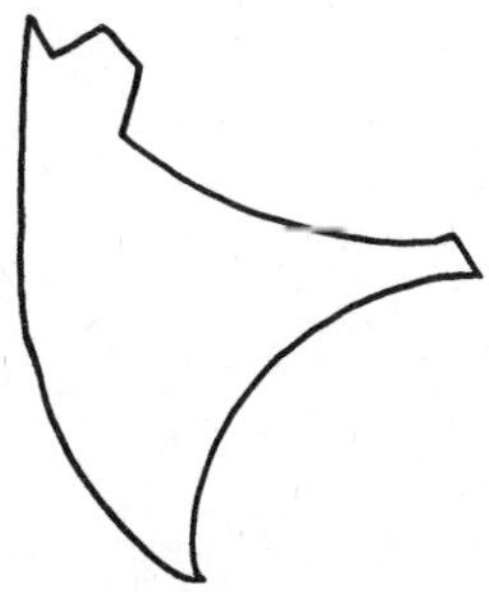

5. At this point, you can paint, color and further decorate your mask. Attach feathers and streamers. Use colors appropriate for your purpose

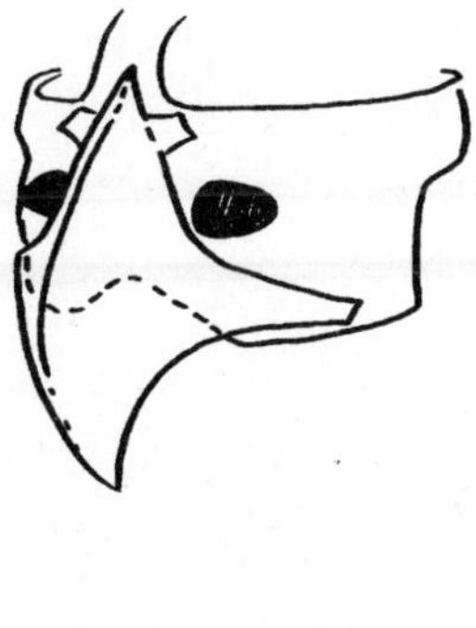

The Owl Mask

1. Draw or photocopy the design and enlarge it so that it will fit over your face. Poster board is heavier and will often work better than just plain paper.

2. Cut out the design and fold the flaps of the beak and attach to the underside of the mask.

3. Select colors and patterns appropriate for the great horned owl, including its beak.

4. Attach small feathers to the face, and especially over the points at the top to reflect the feathery tufts or horns on this owl.

5. Make two small holes on each side of the face at the level of the eyes.

6. Take a piece of ribbon or string and weave in through those slits on each side. This will allow the mask to be tied at the back of the head.

Skill
Development

Awakening the Animal's Power

Benefits:

- **Improves ability to connect with totems**
- **Improves intuitive and creative abilities**
- **Develops strong connections to raven and owl.**

Having a mask, shield and staff can truly help us align with our animal totems more powerfully. We can create processes that will help us shift into the animal's energy and help awaken its energy in us. In time we will find a way that is easiest for you, and you will discover that if you need to, with just simple postures and movements, you can manifest and express the animal's's energy as you need it.

1. Make sure you will not be disturbed.

2. Have your mask available.
If you do not have a mask available, you can use body art, painting the face and body to reflect the animal.

3. Incorporate your shield and staff into the process.
Place them where you can see them and draw upon them for protection and extra energy.

4. Know what your movements will be ahead of time.
Study the animal. Watch nature programs and get videos of the animal. Note how it walks, how it holds its head and how it postures. The more of its natural behaviors that you can incorporate, the stronger the awakening of its energy in you.

5. Have an opening posture.
I have found the one on the left to be very effective. It is a modified horse stance, providing balance and receptivity. It allows movement into new energies.

6. Imitate the movements of the animal.
It doesn't need to be elaborate. Perform it slowly. Take about three to five minutes for this activity. In time you will find it easier to go longer lengths of time, connecting more powerfully to the animal.

7. Now imagine, see and feel the animal coming to you.
Visualize it appearing before you and greet it. I use the following: "My heart to your heart, your heart to my heart. I am honored by you and I thank you for sharing your life with me."

8. See the animal melt into you.
Feel yourself becoming the animal. Feel its energy and qualities coming alive stronger within you with every breath that you take. Visualize how you will be able to apply its qualities to your life. Take about 10 -15 minutes feeling the energy alive within you.

9. Offer thanks to the animals for coming into your life.
I often use the prayer in #6 again at this point. I then visualize the animal moving off to watch and guard from a distance.

10. Perform a grounding posture and some grounding acclivities.
This can be the posture that you used in #5 or the one depicted on the right, which I use to ground. It puts me into solid contact with the earth. Grounding at the end is especially important. It helps prevent disorientation and that "spacey feeling". While in that posture feel your self returning to your human essence, but strengthened by the animal's power and medicine. Afterwards, many find it beneficial to eat something light.

Skill
Development

A Touch of Invisibility

Benefits:

- **Improves ability to work with animals**
- **Improves stillness of the mind**
- **Develops shapeshifting abilities and invisibility**

The idea of being invisibility teases most people. There are so many things we could do. So much fun we could have. Everyone at some point has imagined what it would be like to be invisible.

There are many levels to it and most of us have experienced some form of invisibility. Remember the last time that no one seemed to notice you? That's a form of invisibility. Remember the last time someone tripped over you, saying, "I'm sorry, I didn't see you there." That is a form of invisibility.

As a child I was a bit sickly with very bad asthma, so I was often propped up in a chair in a corner of the room with the adults when there were gatherings and parties. I would become relatively invisible to them. In time I began to enjoy those occasions because I would find out things about those present that I would never have found out otherwise. When you are "not really there", people don't watch what they say.

When we can walk around without being seen and without anyone taking notice – whether we are physically visible or not – we are experiencing invisibility. When we do it at will, we are weaving a magical cloak of invisibility about ourselves.

There is a lot of confusion about the practice of invisibility. It is an aspect of the shapeshifting and the weaving of glamour. It is a skill that takes much practice. With the following exercises you will lay a foundation for the developing of this ability.

1. The key to this exercise is stillness and concentration. Learning to keep the mind still takes practice. Concentration is the art of holding a thought or image that you have created without the mind wandering. Try counting slowly to ten, focusing only on one number at a time. If you find your mind wandering, bring it back to the number.

2. Another way of working with it is to practice being still, not moving and only focusing on one thought or image (preferably yourself as being invisible) while in a group situation. Parties, libraries, and other places people gather can be good places to practice this. Do this for longer and longer periods of time. Start with 30 seconds and then extend it. Visualize yourself as just part of the surroundings, like a piece of furniture.

   Much of this ability is learning to control the aura, the energy surrounding the human body. You can learn to adjust its intensity so that you "blend in". Practice standing against a wall and see yourself and your aura becoming part of the wall, just as if you were fading or melting into it.

3. One of the best ways of developing invisibility is by working with "fox medicine" in Native American traditions. This is an animal that can be three feet from you in the wild and you not know it is there. It knows how to be still and camouflaged.

   Working to blend in with your surroundings, to come and go unnoticed is part of what fox medicine teaches. Working to move silently without revealing your intentions is part of the art of invisibility.

   The fox uses its ability at quiet and stillness for its invisibility. The next time you go to a party, take a seat on the couch or chair, and visualize yourself as a fox that blends in perfectly to the environment. Imagine yourself taking on the pattern and colors of the couch or chair. Then sit quietly and watch how many people accidentally bump into you or even try to sit down on you because they did not "see you". You will be amazed.

4. A variation of #3 is to practice imagining yourself as a fox when you enter or leave a gathering. See yourself as blending into the gathering, melting into it. Do not be surprised as the night goes on that others will make such comments as, "When did you get here?" "How long have you been here?" "I didn't see you come in," or "When did you leave?" The more you work with fox, the easier it becomes.

Notes

Lakota

We love the draft horses. They are big, strong and gentle. We were looking for a special draft horse, one with pinto markings. We had spent a day with a man looking over his horses, but we never found what we liked. He mentioned that he had one more group in another pasture. As we stepped through the fence, we saw the herd at the top of rise about 200 yards away. I heard a soft whisper, "Lakota" and a spotted horse immediately caught our eye. He was muscular and high headed. My wife and I gave each other glances and we continued up the hill.

As we approached, a spotted horse walked easily over to us. He was smaller than the one we saw but with the same markings. This one looked malnourished, borderline starving. He stood and nuzzled us as if we were old friends. As I gave him a good scratch, I looked around for the horse we saw from the bottom of the hill. He was nowhere to be seen. I asked the owner if there were any other spotted drafts in this group and he said that this one was the only one.

It was then I heard, "My name is Lakota." Again it was a soft whisper in my head – the same as before. I realized then that we had been shown a vision of the potential in this horse. We didn't buy him that day, but we both knew that we would likely buy this horse. Neither of us said anything. I didn't mention for several days what I had heard whispered to me. Not because my wife would think I was strange but rather because whenever I hear the name of an animal, it usually becomes ours.

Well, we did buy him, and when he was delivered he was even more malnourished than when we left him. In time though he grew healthier and stronger and has become the horse we saw dancing across the top of the distant hill.

And he is Lakota - friend and ally.

Chapter 9

Animal Communication & Telepathy

Interspecies communication. Animal psychics. Animals talking to people and people talking to animals. Do people really expect others to believe there is some kind of human-animal communication going on? Is it really possible that animals have the cognitive abilities to relate to us? For most people it sounds a little too much like Dr. Doolittle, but the truth is that interspecies communication is a reality.

As children we all believed that animals talked and communicated – to each other and even to us. Most children know when things are wrong with their pets and often bring those communications to the attention of adults. Adults, unfortunately, usually treat them as cute and imaginative, sending a message that what children sense and experience from their animals is not real. And the barriers begin to go up.

Fortunately though, we are living in a time when the barriers are being broken down. People are returning to a part of themselves they had forgotten about. Animal communicators and animal psychics are showing up everywhere and it is a wonderful sign. It marks a growing return to what has been so often ignored in modern society. As people begin to explore their more creative aspects, they find themselves reconnecting to Nature and to animals in new and powerful ways. People are beginning to remember that there is a spirit to everything, regardless of what kind of life form it may be.

One of the most frequent questions I get in workshops and lectures is, "Do you actually talk to animals?" And the answer is, "Yes I do." I have

Horses Say the Darndest things

Ted shares an interlude and amusing conversation with a young filly.

never gone by the terms "animal communicator" or "animal psychic" but I have always communicated with animals. They talk to me. I talk to them. They seek me out – both domestic and wild animals. But I am not that unusual, special or gifted. I do what many others are also doing. And I don't do anything that others can't learn to do as well.

For some people, the childhood barriers never went up. I believe that I was just too stubborn (or too willful, depending upon whom you ask) to believe it when adults told me that what I was experiencing wasn't real, and others are beginning to remember this reality as well. But again I wish to stress that those who communicate with animals are no more gifted than anyone else – except maybe in the fact that we recognize our innate ability to relate to animals as any other creative, cognitive and intelligent being.

Communicating with animals and Nature is something that we all can do. It is a part of our innate potentials as humans. It is natural for us, but as humans in the modern word we have begun to rely solely upon verbal communication and we forget that there are many other ways of communicating. Most people allowed those abilities to atrophy, but the potential is still there. We never lose it.

How Animals Communicate

Animals do communicate and if we wish to communicate with them and have them communicate with us, then we need to understand how they are capable. Think of it like learning a foreign language, one that you knew as a child and now must refresh yourself. Animals communicate in a variety of ways. The most common tools of communication they use are sounds, smells, touch, body language, and thought projection.

Most animals vocalize in some form or fashion. Crows caw to each other with unique rhythms and tones to communicate messages. Canines bark, yip, whine and howl. Cats purr, meow and even trill. And depending upon the particular species of animal the sounds they make will mean different things. Pet rats chitter when they see you as a way of greeting you, showing excitement.

Smell and fragrance is also a part of communication with animals. Many use the smell of waste products to mark territory. Many animals have glandular secretions that invite mating and repel threats. Smells are used to threaten and attract and they are assessed and interpreted accurately by other members of their species.

Touch is a common method of communicating. Horses groom each other as a way of bonding. Cats rub up against you is a way of marking you as part of its family. Some animals greet through licks and even little nips. Biting is used to warn, play and even seduce.

By far the most important form of communication with animals occurs through body language. A white-tailed deer, lifting its tail to flash its white underside, alerts others of the herd to dangers. A horse with its ears flattened back is communicating aggression. Wolves have an intricate and subtle way of communicating through postures and movements. Body language relays information about mood, the environment and more. A kestrel that is kiting – fluttering its wings and hovering – is preparing to make a strike. Behaviors, postures, movements all communicate thoughts, emotions and more. A dog leaping up to greet us is communicating to us that it recognizes us as the alpha. A parrot that regurgitates its food on you is demonstrating its love. It is what parrots do for its mate.

Thought projection or telepathy is another way that animals communicate with each other and with humans. Most animals are telepathic. Their instincts are sharper and more in tune than our own. While we have the luxury of just focusing on the five senses and ignoring the sixth, animals in the wild need that sixth sense to survive. Telepathy can be awakened and developed by each of us without exception. And it is key to communicating with animals effectively.

To communicate with anyone requires that we listen and attend quietly. The same is true of communication with animals. Just as no two people ever communicate quite the same, so too it is with animals. There are some basics techniques that we can develop that will facilitate not only being to relate to animals more effectively but to begin to actually communicate with them.

Begin Communicating with Animals

As we remember our connection to Nature, we soon realize that we can communicate with animals as friends, allies, brothers and sisters. Interspecies communication begins with realizing that all animals have spirits and that all animals communicate through their spirit as well as their bodies. By learning to link with the animal's spirit we open ourselves to wondrous possibilities. Loving pet owners have known this throughout history.

Every loving pet owner knows that his or her pet talks to them. They know that the animal, even though it may not understand the words, does understand the tone and the emotion behind their words. Every pet owner knows that he or she also communicates in unspoken ways with the animal. Whether we call it intuition, telepathy, understanding of subtle body language – it doesn't matter. What matters is that there is communication going on.

The first step to communicating with any animal is to quiet the mind. Learn to relax. Perform some meditation, or relaxation process to help you. We live in a society in which our senses are overstimulated. We need to still the mind so that we can recognize the soft communications from animals. I have found Tai Chi to be very effective and it is now being recommended for those individuals working with horses that are a bit high strung. Leave the outside world outside for the brief time you are connecting with the animal. It will all be waiting for you when you are done.

For domestic animals and pets, I prefer to touch them. The physical connection for me is important in the communication process. I do not have to touch them throughout the process, but some physical contact initially helps to bring our energies into harmony. Our auras begin to blend and mix. With wild animals, this is rarely possible and not recommended except under controlled situations. Having done wildlife rescue and rehab, there are opportunities for this but it is unusual because the stress levels of the animals are higher, usually because injury is involved.

I also use my voice when connecting with the animals. I speak softly and slowly. I do not speak continuously as this can get very distressful for some animals. I keep emotions out of my voice and I lower it in tone. It is calming and soothing and the animals respond to it.

As you sit with the animal, pay attention to behaviors and the body language of the animal. Is the behavior normal? Exaggerated? Unusual? Is there something about the facial expression that is catching your attention? What does the animal's posture say to you?

As you attend to the behaviors and body language, examine what emotions you are feeling. Are there certain emotions coming to the forefront? Pay attention to physical feelings as well? Are there any sensations in any part of your body? When we are starting to connect with the animal, the connection will often trigger an emotional or physical response. It can be very subtle, but if you have relaxed and stilled the mind, you will notice it.

Animals are empathic. They sense and feel the emotional states of those around them. This includes other animals and humans. They know if we are tense, angry, or sad. When we start to connect with them we will have empathic responses to them as well. We will sense and often feel their emotions – as if they are our own. We have several feral cats that were rescued, and although they have been part of the household for five years, they are still very aloof. They stay around us in the house, but they do not like a lot human contact. Occasionally they have to go for their vet visit. By the time they are gathered for the visit, my adrenaline is extremely high and my heart is pounding. I know it is in response to what they are feeling. Note the emotion but do not dwell on it.

When you are relaxed and comfortable with the animal. Reach out with your mind and mentally ask the animal if there is something it would like to share with you. I find that with domestic animals it helps to softly speak their name and question. With wild animals I will use "friend Crow" or "Sister Hawk" or some such phrase.

Then I close my eyes and pay attention to whatever comes to mind. Some may say that this part is nothing more than imagination and my answer is usually, "Yes, it is." Imagination is not the same as being unreal. Imagination is the image-making faculty of the brain. It takes what cannot be verbalized and makes a picture of it for us.

The communication comes to us the way any psychic message comes to us. Sometimes it is an image. Sometimes it is like watching a video. Sometimes it is audible, like hearing a voice in your head. Sometimes it is just a feeling or impression – vague but still there. It is not always going to be immediately clear, especially when we are starting out. Be patient. We live in a fast food society and everyone wants everything quick and easy..

One way of testing your reception of the message from your pet is to speak it back to the pet and see how the animal responds. You will know whether it is right or wrong by the animal's behavior. Any response is good in the beginning because the lines of communication are being connected, even if they aren't fully functional yet.

Getting a communication is actually the easy part. Understanding and translating the communication so that it is comprehended takes a little more work. You may simply be impressed with an image, but then you have to figure out what that image means and how it applies. This comes with time and practice.

Have fun with the process. Don't be looking for instantaneous, Dr. Doolittle types of responses. Doubts will cause blockage and strengthen barriers. Later we will explore how to remember your own telepathic experiences (and yes, you have had them) and how to begin developing it so that you can communicate with animals more clearly. Have fun with the learning. Don't worry about proving and disproving. It's like learning a new language and everyone learns at their own speed.

Domestic Versus Wild

For most people it will be the domestic animal – particularly the pet – that opens the door to interspecies communication. Most people have more contact with pets and domestic animals than they do the wild animals. Pets and domestics are more used to humans and our strange behaviors and thinking processes. Pets and domestic animals often serve as links to their wild counterparts. Once we learn to connect with the domestic, it becomes easier to connect with the wild.

The process is the same, except it is even more important to be relaxed. Wild animals are more alert and unusual sounds and movements, no matter how slight, will cause them to leave. Survival is critical to their life. Domestic animals do not have that intense survival instinct anymore.

Avoid direct eye contact. It is usually considered aggressive. Predators have eyes that are located on the head like ours, facing forward. Prey animals have eyes located a bit more peripherally so they can be more alert to dangers from all directions. Most animals will see humans as predators at first glance. Direct eye contact is threatening. Glances are fine but staring will put them off.

Contact with them is usually more distant and it is more difficult to make a good connection. Relax. See and feel yourself as part of the environment. If you disturbed it coming in, sit quietly for about ten minutes and birds and other animals frightened off will usually return.

With wild animals it is always a good practice to try and see and feel through the eyes of the animal. Visualize yourself as the animal. Visualize yourself looking out through its eyes and its perspective.

A golden eagle talks with Ted

Barriers to Communicating with Animals

"They Are Just Dumb Creatures"

People usually believe that animals have no cognitive abilities or intelligence. The problem is that we cannot determine an animal's intelligence. We do not have standardized test to give to animals like we do humans to determine levels of intelligence. And it wouldn't be very successful anyway. By observation alone though, we know that many animals are problem solvers. They are good at assessing difficulties of tasks before them and they can read the signs of danger and safety within their environments. Even simple communication is possible with the most rudimentary intelligence- whether human or animal.

"They Can't Speak"

Obviously there is a language barrier. Humans use verbal communication as their primary tool for relating to others, but animals are not verbal with each other. Many humans think that if an animal can't speak then it must have no intelligence and no spirit. They don't use words and sentences as we do, but they vocalize communications that express all emotions and a tremendous variety of thoughts. Many people believe that if it does not involve words it is not a communication, but there are many ways of communicating other than through words. We cannot use the same criteria we use to judge human communication abilities to judge animal communication abilities. It's like assuming that a Russian who does not speak English is not capable of communicating, unless you or the Russian find a common language. When it comes to communicating with animals, we must find a language that is common to us.

"They Have No Spirit"

The word "animal" comes from the Latin "anima", meaning "spirit or breath of life". Many people believe that animals have no souls or spirit, but everything that has been created has some spirit associated with it. All life has form and spirit, and like humans all animals communicate through body and spirit. It may not be the spirit in the same sense as traditional religious doctrine teaches, but it is spirit nonetheless. You do not have to believe that all animals have a creative intelligence, but you should at least be able to accept at some point in your explorations that some archetypal energy or spiritual force is working through the animal. If you are patient and open yourself to the possibility, you will soon discover the spirit of the animal and you will never look upon animals and Nature the same way again.

Let's Look at Telepathy

Telepathy is the ability to send and receive messages and information through the mind. It is mind to mind communications. Sometimes those communications are just thoughts, sometimes they are emotions and sometimes they are physical sensations.

Telepathy can be spontaneous. It can just happen - particularly with those we are close to. If you have ever thought the same thing at the same time as someone else, you have experienced spontaneous telepathy. If you ever knew who was phoning you before picking up the phone, you have experienced spontaneous telepathy. If you have ever felt an ache/pain of a friend when they weren't around, you've experienced spontaneous telepathy.

Although most of us have experienced spontaneous telepathy some time in our lives. It can also be learned and the communication deliberate. These telepathic messages may be in the form of thoughts, feelings or even physical sensations. As you work to develop this skill, you will find that although we each can learn to send and receive, some of you will be better senders and some will be better receivers.

Telepathy – in whatever forms it takes – works best if the emotions are involved. We often hear stories of parents who experience a psychic link with their children. If something happens to the child, they just "know" it. This is a form of emotional or sympathetic telepathy. Lovers often experience this same thing. If you are developing it with someone with whom you share strong emotions, you will have more success in the beginning. The emotions give a power boost to the thoughts.

There is no need to fret though if you do not have a close friend or family member to practice and develop this psychic power with. Later we will discuss ways in which you can develop your telepathic skills with your pets. You can even do it by yourself to some degree, sending and receiving messages from yourself, like giving yourself a wake-up call.

TELEPATHY is
mind to mind communication.

Messages can be:
MENTAL
(sending or experiencing thoughts),
EMOTIONAL / SYMPATHETIC
(sending or experiencing feelings)
PHYSICAL
(sending or experiencing sensations)

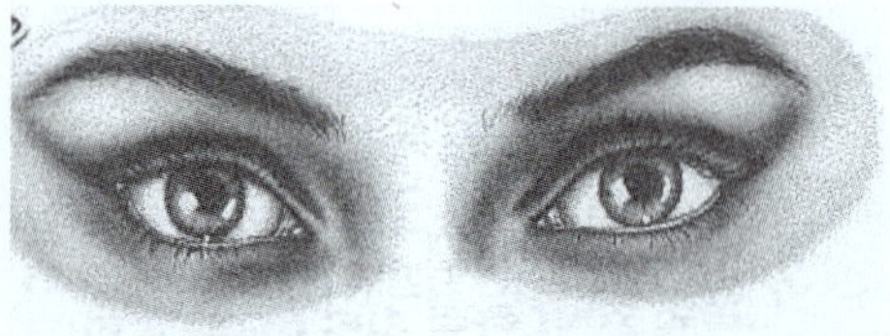

Do You Have Telepathic Ability?

Telepathy is something we can all develop. We often develop psychic and telepathic links with people we are close to. Emotional closeness opens psychic channels. We sense and feel things more easily with those who are closer and more intimate to us. This questionnaire will help you to remember if you have had a telepathic experience with a friend, a member of the family or even a romantic love.

1. Have you ever known what another person is thinking and feeling at times without any verbal communication?

2. Do you seem to instinctively know when good or bad news is coming another person's way?

3. Have you ever experienced sympathetically minor aches or pains at the same time another person was experiencing discomfort?

4. When traveling or just away from a friend or loved one, were you sometimes able to know if he or she was having difficulty and wanted to call you?

5. Have you ever known what friend or loved one has done during the day while you were separate without any prior knowledge or hints?

6. Has another person sometimes acted on your unspoken desires or wishes within a short while after you have been focused upon them yourself or vice versa?

7. Do you and other people ever say the same things at the same time?

8. Have you ever sensed when another person was hiding feelings or thoughts, and later discovered that you were correct?

9. Do you find it difficult to truly surprise other people or vice versa?

10. Can you tell when another person is talking or thinking about you?

The Telepathy Game

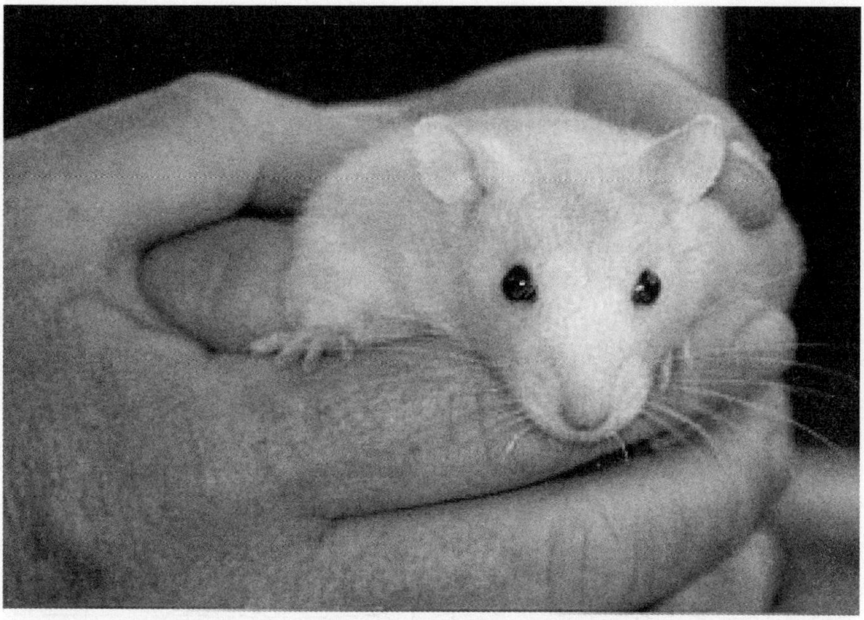

What is Ali Baba the rat thinking?

How about these guinea pigs, Bib and Lucky?

Foundation for Pet Telepathy

All animals sense subtle changes in the environment around them. They are extremely sensitive to emotions. This sensitivity helps make pets great assistants in developing your own telepathic abilities. Working with animals is one of the easiest ways of developing your telepathic skills. The key though is remembering that the stronger the relationship, the stronger the telepathic connection.

The following are ways to lay the foundation for telepathic links with pets and other domestic animals. Wild animals are a different matter and techniques with them are a little more difficult, but if you develop telepathy with your pet, it will be easier to do so later with wild animals.

1. Spend time with your animals.

I can't say it often enough. The stronger the relationship you have with a person or an animal, the stronger your telepathic connection will be.

I have always been good with animals. I am typical of those in the past that were said to "have a way with animals". I'm not sure exactly why this is. I have my own theories which I may explore some other time. But I realized years ago that when I began doing regular obedience training with my dogs the telepathic communication strengthened tremendously.

It was the time spent learning with the dog. It learned about my voice and touch. It came to understand the subtleties of my gestures and postures. It learned how I thought. And I came to know it as well.

Every dog is different and responds uniquely to obedience commands. Some require a firm approach, some a more playful. The training developed a rapport with the dog. I was able to understand more fully the personality and essence of the dog and it could understand mine. This made it easier to use telepathy with them.

Cats are much more independent than dogs and with them it is the early playtime and regular touching of the animal that establishes the connection. It is very difficult to develop telepathy with a cat that has not been touched or petted much. In the early months this is most critical.

Playtime is also most essential when working with animals. If you do not have playtime with your animals there is not going to be much of a telepathic link.

Even the training should be treated as fun. Everything is easier if we enjoy doing it. Playtime for animals is as essential for them as it is for humans. Without it we become crotchety and self-centered, and this blocks psychic perceptions.

Spending time to play and work with your pets helps build a psychic link with them. This link then becomes the foundation for developing telepathic communication with them.

2. Never force connections.

Let the animal set the tone and rhythm. Connections should never be forced. With animals the connection – especially of trust – must be established before the telepathy truly begins.

A number of years ago I was doing a workshop on my book ANIMAL-SPEAK. One of the participants brought a dog that had been ill, hoping that I would do some healing work on it. People at the workshop got up and started rushing over to the dog, oohing and ahhing. I felt a lot of it was a show - to demonstrate to me that they were true animal people.

The dog tried to get away and finally hid in the back. I didn't do anything. I didn't even approach the dog. As the workshop went on the dog began to edge closer. By the end of the seminar, the dog was laying next to my bag underneath the table up front.

Connections should never be forced. They should be allowed to happen. It is always best to let the animal approach you. Animals are more sensitive and need to feel comfortable. I cannot count how many times in my life I have been told not to get upset if a particular animal does not take to me, that "It's not friendly" or "it only likes a few people". Inevitably the animal does come to me, lays on my feet or crawls up on my lap. But I never force. I send comforting, thoughts of safety toward them and they respond accordingly. Telepathy works best if there is genuine trust and safety between the partners – whether person to person or person to animal.

The stronger the relationship,

The stronger the telepathic connection!

Do Animals Have Souls?

A woman died and was brought before God. God looked at her and asked, "Do you know why you will be permitted into heaven?"

The woman replied, "Because in spite of all my failings, I have tried to be a good person?"

"No", said God. "Do you remember when you were walking home from work and you came across a cat, creeping along and weak – almost dying - from the cold? Out of pity you picked it up and wrapped it inside of the coat you were wearing, to protect it from the cold. Because you showed such mercy for that cat, I have had mercy on you."

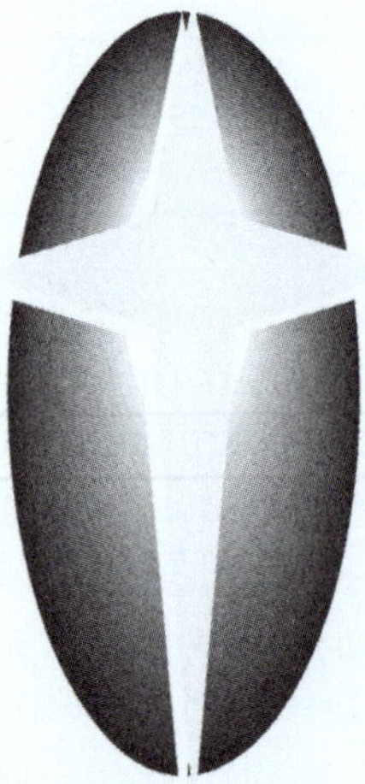

I am often asked in workshops whether or not I believe animals have souls. And the truth is I do, although religious sources will often disagree. Many religions teach that animals do not live on after death – that they don't have a soul or spirit. They are not as important as humans are even if God did create them.

From my experience, animals do have souls. And some even return as ghosts, especially those with whom we have bonded. Animals display intelligence, caring and nurturing – and often better than humans - including myself. And their spirit is just as strong as humans, even if it is not as developed in the way human spirit is or even if it is just plain different.

Skill
Development

Establishing Lines of Communication

Benefits:

- **Develops telepathy**
- **Lays foundation for communicating with animals**
- **Helps in locating lost animals**

In the past 5-10 years, more and more animal communicators have appeared on the scene. In general animal communicators are those who usually either telepathically communicate with the spirit of the animal or perform psychic readings of various types by tuning into a person's pet.

This exercise has a variety of applications. There are ways it can be used to lay the foundation for becoming an animal communicator. It can also be adapted to locate and call missing pets back to us – when it is possible for them to do so. Do not be afraid to experiment. When performed outdoors, it can be used to call your spirit animal or totem to you.

Some will say that we don't need to go through all of this connecting and hooking up of energy centers to communicate with animals. And they are right ...kind of. Most people just learning need specific steps - need some logical flow to help bridge to that more subtle communications. This exercise provides this.

1. Make your preparations.
Make sure that you are in a different room from your dog or cat. Create a sacred space, a space that is quiet and relaxed. Perform a progressive relaxation. The more still and calm you are, the more effective it is.

2. Prepare to make a special energy hook-up to your pet.
Those who are metaphysically minded will recognize this as a chakra hook-up. We are going to establish lines of energy between our pet and us. I have

found that four connections are effective – the crown, heart, the base of the spine (base of the tail) and the feet. As you make each connection, whisper or speak softly the name of your pet.

3. Start linking your energy to your pet.
Start with visualizing a soft beam of light from the crown of your head connecting with the crown of your pet. Then connect your heart to the heart of the animal. See and feel the gentle light connection between you and your pet. (Some people find that connecting the solar plexus area to a similar position on the animal is more effective than the heart. The solar plexus center in humans is linked to our emotions, and animals respond strongly to emotions. It is a most powerful center to link with animals.) Try both and see which gets the best response. Then continue to the base of the spine, linking your primal energies to the pet. See it as a soft, gentle and strong connection to a point at the base of the animals tail region. The last hook up is a bit different. We have smaller chakra centers in the arches of our feet and the palms of our hands, and we should link them with the feet of our pet.

4. Once the connection is made, visualize your pet coming to visit you.
Feel it excited to see you and you excited to see it. Imagine it coming into where you are sitting. Call it to you softly in your mind.

5. Continue this for about 5 minutes or until the pet arrives.
When it does, make sure you reward it with some wonderful petting and loving. Thank it for coming to you, for responding to your thoughts. Do not be discouraged if it doesn't happen at first. End the exercise, thanking the spirits for helping, if only to assist in making your pet more receptive.

6. Go and find your animal.
When you find it, take note of what it is doing. Has it moved at all since you started the exercise? Is it closer to you?

7. Take some time here and give your pet some loving attention.
Sometimes the process is confusing to the animal, and it is not sure what to do. Your petting it helps to let it know that it is OK to visit you when it hears the call.

Animal Ambassadors

Everytime I am in a group that is talking about animal totems and animal spirits, I am surprised at how many people tell me their totem is a wolf or a dolphin. Is this unusual? Are they just attaching themselves to an animals that is glamorous or is there something else going on?

People do share the same totems. There are a lot of people working with the same animals, but each person has to develop a unique relationship with that animal. The red-tailed hawk is one of my totems. I have worked with them both hands-on and in spirit for many years, but there are many people working with the hawk. How I work with and use the hawk medicine can be different from others. And that is as it should be. Each person must find a way of incorporating and applying the animal's qualities and energies into their own unique life circumstances.

In the United States, we all share a totem - the bald eagle. As citizens of this country we are aligned in some way with this animal and thus must find some way of working with it in our life.

On the other hand there are animals that seem to act as ambassadors for others in the animal kingdom. They capture the imagination and reawaken interest. Animal spirits like the dolphin and wolf can do this much easier than the spirit of the slug or the weasel. Wolf and dolphin often serve as ambassadors.

I think it is important to examine animals more closely that seem to capture the public's attention. Usually they have a message for society as a whole. When we study the wolf and the dolphin, we can find strong similarities. They are both mammals but they live in entirely different environments, hinting that no matter what environment you live in or come from there is something you can learn from them.

Both animals live in groups. The dolphin lives in a pod and the wolf lives in a pack. Both are extremely intelligent and sociable animals. Both have great skills at working together to survive. Both have intricate vocal language and body language. They are tremendous communicators.

Maybe the reason that they capture society's attention is to remind us that cooperation and communication are the two most important qualities for success in today's world. They remind us that we each have a role in society, even as we develop our individuality.

Stewards of the Earth

Long before there was a long ago, the dragon was the guardian of the animals. He was the greatest and most powerful animal and humans were afraid of him. It was this alone, which prevented most humans from harming animals. Unfortunately, as the ages passed, humans quit believing in dragons. Because they no longer believed, they no longer feared the dragon.

More and more animals began to be harmed. Many species disappeared altogether. Nature was being hurt and disrespected. And the dragon was saddened by all of this. He could no longer do his job. So he decided it was time to leave.

The dragon was married to the phoenix. She was the great bird of rebirth who rose from her own ashes. She saw his great sorrow. As much as she tried though, she could not console him. She knew that once his mind was set, he would not change it. But then she had an idea and so she waited and watched.

Discouraged and frustrated, the dragon prepared to give up his guardianship. If people did not believe, thee was no reason for him to stay. So he faced the sun, and he inhaled his own fire and that of the sun. He began to swell, growing larger and larger and then he exploded into millions of pieces. The phoenix watched with great love and sorrow and as he exploded, she allowed herself to go up in flames. A great wind caught her ashes and swirled them amidst the pieces of dragon. And they attached themselves. As each ash touched a piece of the dragon, there was a flash of fire and a beautiful red-tailed hawk was born, soaring across the sky.

To this day, this red-tailed hawk sits perched, watching the world. Born of dragon and phoenix, its spirit is now the true guardian of the animal world, and whenever seen perched high upon a tree or pole, it is a reminder of the guardianship of the dragon and phoenix, alive within the hawk and still alive within the world.

Those who became guardians of Nature, protectors of animals and Steward of the Earth, would come to be known as Dragonhawks.

Chapter 10

Sacred Journeys

In more ancient societies the shamans were the keepers of sacred knowledge of animals and Nature. They were held in high esteem and recognized as true shapeshifters. They were able to walk the worlds. They were linked to the rhythms and forces of nature.

Shamanism is an experiential growth process. It involves becoming the master of your own initiation. In shamanism the individual ultimately answers to no human or totem and is alone with the supernatural. Yet he or she maintains a true sense of belonging and connectedness to all life. This individual is able to visit the heavens and the underworld. This individual is able to learn from all life forms.

A person usually becomes a shaman by one of three methods:

- By inheriting the profession,
- By a special calling, or
- By a personal quest.

The process of following that personal quest and unfolding the innate powers begins with two steps. The first is the overcoming of preconceived notions and limitations. There is as much unlearning to do as there is learning.

The most difficult part of this step is seeing through the illusions of our lives. Becoming the shaman practitioner develops a strong sense of not truly belonging to reality. We are often taught that we should belong to something. Many people spend their whole lives attempting to belong. Most of the time it leads to disappointment. The animal-wise shaman must develop an individuality that is strong. Through the animals we learn that we are able to be alone without being lonely.

There are no temples or shrines among us save those of nature. Being children of nature, we are intensely poetical. We would deem it sacrilege to build a house for The One who may be met face to face in the mysterious, shadowy aisles of the primeval forest, or on the sunlit bosom of virgin prairies, upon dizzy spires and pinnacles of naked rock, and in the vast jeweled vault of the night sky!

A God who is enrobed in filmy veils of cloud, there on the rim of the visible world where our Great-Grandfather Sun kindles his evening camp fire; who rides upon the rigorous wind of the north, or breathes forth spirit upon fragrant southern airs, whose war canoe is launched upon majestic rivers and inland seas - such a God needs no lesser cathedral.

- Ohiyesa

Another important step in the shaman quest is building a bridge between our world and the more subtle realms of life. This involves unfolding our intuition, creativity, and creative imagination. The individual learns to visit the heavens and the underworld by means of an axis. The axis may be the image of climbing a tree, being carried or led by an animal, by becoming a bird or animal, following a cave through a labyrinth or any number of other possible images. Ancient societies employed mythic imagination to facilitate this step.

We must now move beyond the orthodox treatment of mythic imagery (including that of animals) as found in modern religion. In today's world these images and their association to outer reality are held in fixed, unchangeable dogma. They have grown stale. They have lost their ability to touch each of us uniquely. We must restore the experiential aspect to the mythic images of life and transform our usual perceptions through an epiphany with Nature.

Tools for the Shamanic Quest

Every shamanic tradition has its own rituals, music, myths and sacred dances. Each tradition had its own means of awakening practitioners to the powerful forces and magic of Nature. Nature teaches us that all life is change. Everything is in a state of transition. All change, all crises, all sacrifice, all death and all birth reflect the archetypal power in Nature. The shamanic practitioner uses rituals and tools to align with these energies and manifest them within his or her life. The most common tools are musical instruments and shamanic dance.

Musical Instruments

Three instruments in particular are powerful tools for the shamanic practitioner. They do not require any previous musical knowledge and they can be used for a wide variety of magical and meditative practices. Those on spiritual and shamanic journeys will find them powerful tools.

Drum

Rhythm is the pulse of life and it affects all physical energies. It is the heartbeat and drums enable connection to the heartbeat of animals and the heartbeat of Mother Earth. Rhythms quicken, slow and change heart rates and organs of the body associated with it. Many shamanic practices involve riding the drumbeat to alter states of consciousness and to induce trance conditions. It is used to slow the heart rhythm or to stimulate a change in the heart rhythm to be more resonant with a particular animal. It was almost unthinkable for an ancient shaman, medicine person or healer not to have a drum or a rhythm instrument.

Depending upon the syncopation, or the pauses within the rhythms, specific physiological affects could be generated. In shamanic storytelling, the drum is used to bring the audience into resonance with each other and with the energies of the story. It can be used to align with the rhythms and energies of specific animals. Voudoun, a Haitian religion, does not attempt to disguise the use of the drum for stimulating specific kinds of energies. The drum is used to block out the rational mind, activate sexual energies and to induce trance. The incessant rhythmic drumming triggers a forced resonance in the participant, altering normal heart rhythms to elicit contact with primal forces.

Rattle

The rattle is also a rhythmic instrument and like its mate the drum, it is one of the oldest healing instruments. The rattle and its rhythms have a capacity for linking the waking consciousness to the energies of the cosmos or to levels of consciousness deep within. It serves to release energy and power for healing and cleansing.

Its use as a shamanic healing instrument is widespread. The rhythmic sounds of the rattle loosen rigid energy patterns around the body, promoting healing and balance. It has been used in a variety of ways, but in most traditions, it was used while encircling the body of person. Then the rattle is shaken up and down the front and back of the body.

Many rattles of the past were made from dried gourds with seeds placed in them. Some were made from dried bones. And even those who believe they have no sense of rhythm has the ability to use a rattle without any musical knowledge. We can begin to experiment with the rattle and our own energies.

Flute

The flute and whistle is an old shamanic tool. It has existed in various forms in different societies and traditions. It is considered one of the first instruments to enable humanity to connect with the beings of Nature – the faeries, elves, devas and others. It is powerfully effective when used in shamanic and magical storytelling. And it was commonly used as a way of calling specific spirits – including those of the animal kingdom.

The flute is considered an extension of the body. It is played with the breath of life, a true creative force. It can be used to connect with the consciousness of Nature. There are many types that are easy to play, whether you are familiar with music or not. It can be used to create your own musical calls to the spirit world.

Shamanic Dance

Dance and movement is one of the most powerful shamanic tools. It awakens and stirs the energies of life. True sacred dance is a means of focusing and directing consciousness through physical behavior. When incorporated with mask making and shapeshifting practices, it becomes a powerful force for transformation. We can create simple dances of protection, as invitation to spirits, for attunement to animals and for empowering any aspect of life.

Dance and movement is natural to the universe. Plants move in graceful and rhythmic ways. They turn to face the sun; they wave in the breeze; they grow in spiral and other exquisite forms. Birds have their own movements and dances, spreading their wings and plumage in magnificent displays of courtship and strength. All animals have unique dances and movements to show strength, aggression, attraction or just high-spirited fun.

The human body is designed for movement. It is as natural and important to life as breathing. Like breathing, it fills us with energy. It enables us to transcend our usual perceptions and consciousness. Movement balances, heals, awakens, and energizes. It generates psychic energy for strength, for enlightenment, for life and even for death.

Dance and movement links the hemispheres of the brain, joining the intuitive with the rational. Directed physical behavior, like dance, can help us overcome our tendency to over-rationalize and block our own growth process. It aligns our physical responses and energies with our spiritual goals and helps us to maintain contact with the higher forces of life.

Shamanic dance should be performed as a way of reaching another level of consciousness or being. It should be a way of releasing spiritual meaning into our lives. Dance ritual is not meant to be performed for audiences, which profanes it in many ways. We must participate in and become the priests, priestesses, shamans and medicine people of the ritual. Participation in shamanic dance requires us to remember that energies are not created by the dance but simply invoked, challenged and directed by it. We must remember that the energies function less through our talent for dancing than through our participation. Thus anyone who can move any part of his or her body can create and participate in a shamanic or magickal dance – even if only through the flickering of the eyes or the rhythm of the breath.

Shamanic and magickal dance can be performed by anyone. No formal training is required to utilize the powerful effects of dance. Dances for higher states of consciousness are simple, individual and passionate. They do not require great space, for when a dance pattern is created for special effects, it will create an illusion of great space. Dances to attune to animals require little more than imitating their movements and postures. It is simply a matter of imbuing movement with greater significance and focus. It is not the talent that invokes the energy but the participation. With just a little effort, you will find yourself dancing between worlds. Your sacred journey will become empowered and more sacred than you ever imagined.

Skill
Development

Animal Guardians & Psychic Protection

Benefits:

- **Develops skill at handling opposition**
- **Lays foundation for working with animals**
- **Helps in psychic protection**

Every animal in Nature has behaviors that it uses to protect itself and to defend its territory. Sometimes it's part of its adaptation. Some animals have physical adaptations, and some animals have behavioral adaptations. Physical adaptations are like the bright colors found on some insects as a warning to predators that if they try and eat them it will leave a bad taste in their mouth. Some caterpillars have white spots or blotches on their backs that resemble the splatter of bird poop. Since their most common predator is a bird, this is a physical adaptation that will help prevent birds from eating them. A bird will never eat something that has been pooped on. Some animals in Nature have behavioral adaptations. Some, such as rabbits, have a wonderful ability to remain still if they feel danger is close by. Most predators recognize prey by movement, so a rabbit's ability to freeze is an adaptive behavior for avoiding becoming someone's meal.

We do need to remember that *every* animal, from a tiny mouse to an eagle, has ways of defending itself and protecting its home. They all have their own unique abilities for defense and protection. Do not assume that a large predator is what you should work with in psychic protection, you will probably find yourself in for an interesting educational lesson. Most people would think that a hawk would have no trouble with a rabbit, and yet jackrabbits have been known to drag hawks, who have sunk their talons into the rabbits back, into their holes and then kick them to death.

A great horned owl is one of the most powerful and aggressive birds of prey. A single crow may not be able to handle it, but a flock of crows will mob an owl to drive it away. If we are working with crows to defend and protect ourselves, we will be ineffective if we do it by ourselves. The crow teaches us to join with others.

If we learn how our spirit animal or totem defends itself, we can then apply it to our own life. That animal has shown up to be a part of our life, to tell us," These behaviors I have are what will work for you right now. Use them!" When we do, we find everything coming together and falling into place. We find it easier to accomplish our goals with less trouble.

1. **Begin by choosing an animal to help with your protection.**

We have spoken about how to determine your own spirit animals and totems. Choose one of these, If you are not sure, choose an animal that you always felt drawn to. Or choose an animal that is appearing in your life right now.

If you do not know your spirit animal, meditate on the problem and then take a walk in nature for about an hour. It can be a park or some other natural environment where there is wildlife. Usually by the end of that walk, some animal has gotten our attention, several times. If unsure, wait 24 hours. Within 24 hours that animal will have shown itself 3-4 times around you. You may see it outside, or on a TV program, but there will be three to four encounters.

2. **Study the animal.**

Go to the library and learn as much about that animal as possible. Jot down who its predators are and whom it preys upon. Most animals in the wild fall within the middle, being both predators and prey.

Study how it defends its home. This is the most important part. Does it do it alone? Does it have help? Does it hide? Does it camouflage itself? How does it defend and protect itself? This animal has gotten your attention to teach you how to apply these same tactics to your life.

If you have someone or something troubling you, this animal's natural tactics will help. If it is an opossum, you might have to develop some play acting skills around certain individuals so they do not know your business or what is truly going on. Some animals put on an intense show of strength and power as a warning to intruders. If we have people or even spirits that are aggravating us, we may have to put on a stronger display and assert greater control. Find a way of applying the animal's natural defense tactics to our individual situation.

3. Examine where you are having difficulty.

Make a list of people that may be troubling you, or of whom you may have suspicions. Are there certain phenomena that are unsettling? Are you feeling unbalanced? Write down the ideas. As you are doing this focus on the animal and its behavior. Ask yourself how this animal would handle such a situation? Would it hide until the trouble goes away and passes? Would it camouflage itself? Would it confront with a display of ferocity? Would it join with others of its kind to handle the situation? The animal is the solution.

4. Join with the animal.

Find a time when you will not be disturbed – preferably outdoors if possible. Visualize the animal appearing before you, its eyes looking into your eyes. As it does, you realize that this creature has your eyes – that it is your eyes looking out of it at you.

As you realize this, the animal melts into you. With each breath that you take, its essence grows stronger inside of you. You feel as it feels. Your senses are alive. As this animal grows stronger within you, you see yourself handling all of the problems in the same way this animal would. Allow your imagination to run with it.

Although it may seem as if its a fanciful past time, the effects will be very real over the next three days. Opportunities to correct situations that are out of balance will arise. The tactics that this animal would use are what will work for you.

Skill
Development

The Power of Predator and Prey

Benefits:

- **Develops assertiveness with problems**
- **Lays foundation for strong protection & guardianship**
- **Helps sharpen senses in issues of trust and distrust**

Predators and prey are found everywhere in nature. A predator is defined as one who has the ability to take live prey. There has always been a contest between predator and prey in the natural world, and life is always the prize. The grasshopper eats the grass and the frog eats the grasshopper. The snake eats the frog and the hawk eats the snake.

Predation takes time, patience and skill. It sharpens the senses. The strongest, most alert and knowledgeable will survive. Animals grow stronger and wiser trying to avoid being caught.

This simple meditation/visualization is a powerful tool for protection. It may seem simple, but in its simplicity, it has even greater effectiveness. For this exercise though you will need to choose a predator animal. This may be an animal that you know is already one of your totems. It may be an animal that you have always had an affinity for. It may be an animal that you have dreamt of. It may be an animal that you choose out of the blue.

Only spend 5-10 minutes a day on this exercise, but put a lot of passion into it. Within a week, you will begin to notice a difference. Problems and stresses will begin to ease up. Psychic imbalances will settle. Make sure that you see yourself stronger, healthier and more empowered as a result of this exercise.

1. Choose your predator and study it.

Again, go to the library and learn something about the animal. How does it attack and defend? What kind of natural weapons and skills does it have? When hunting, what skills does it rely upon?

What is its most common prey? In other words, what animal does it eat? What tactics will its prey most likely use to avoid being caught? (This is most important. By understanding how the prey is more likely to respond, by understanding how it naturally behaves, we can use that to our advantage.)

2. Prepare for the meditation.

Make sure that you will be undisturbed. The phone should be off the hook. You might want to use a candle or fragrance to enhance the meditation. Perform a progressive relaxation. The more relaxed you are the more effective it will be.

3. Visualize a bad habit, an uncomfortable situation or something negative around you as the natural prey.

4. Visualize yourself as the predator.

See yourself sitting out in nature and this predator stepping out in front of you. It fixes you with its eyes, and you realize that it has your eyes. Your eyes are looking out of it at you! As you realize this, it melts into you, and with each breath you see and feel yourself as this predator. It does not just live within you and you in it. You are the predator.

5. Hunt, capture and eat your prey.

Visualize the prey before you, and with the hunting tactics of the predator you are, you attack. See and feel yourself capturing, killing and eating the bad habit, negative attitude, the unbalanced psychic energy, etc. – eliminating it from your life. You become stronger as a result.

Use the predator's natural hunt cycle and tactics in this meditation. If it hunts primarily at night and by stalking, perform the exercise at night. If it hunts during the day, perform it during the day.

The Silent Walk

The silent walk is a powerful exercise for attuning to Nature and the myriad of wonders within it. It is potentially the most powerful exercise we can perform. It is an act of sacred sharing, honor and openness.

The skill lies in walking in silence, abandoning all words, vocalizations, and any trappings of civilization that are likely to make unnatural noises. The silence and harmony of this activity, especially when performed at dawn or dusk, creates an increasing awareness that we share the world with all living things. And ultimately, it will gift us with animal encounters that fill our hearts with blessed wonder.

This exercise should be performed at dawn or dusk because these are sacred times, times in which the spiritual and physical intersect. They are times when the human and the animal walk through similar corridors. They are times in which animals are often more active and visible.

Prepare for this by giving yourself at least a half-hour of meditation time prior to the walk. The focus should be on quiet attunement to Nature. Choose a location that is somewhat secluded – where there will be no traffic. Old country roads that are seldom traveled and overgrown are good. Choose a park or nature center that has trails that are easily followed. Plan on walking a half-hour to forty-five minutes out and then turn around and come back.

Animals sense the energy of a single person or a group, thus the preparatory and solitary meditation. Animals recognize disharmony and even unconscious and unintentional disrespect. If they feel a peace, a harmony that is soft and unthreatening, they do not run away. They do not hide. The animals experienced may move away at your approach, but they do so without the frantic fear that they demonstrate most often when humans approach. They will retreat a few steps at a time, stopping to look over their shoulders, just to satisfy their curiosity.

It is important to continue on at these times slowly and calmly, or if you do pause, resist staring and avoid any broad or sudden movements. Keep the eyes lowered and do not look directly at the animals. Staring will be interpreted as a threatening posture. If we avoid this, we will increasingly sense a growing kinship with the animals. Remember that we are entering their world - not as outsiders or possessors of the land but as distant relatives – cohabitants.

This exercise requires control, sensitivity and a subtle appreciation. It will enhance attunement to the presence of animals not readily encountered or readily visible. Through experiencing Nature in silence we discover everything is an expression of the Divine Life – including ourselves.

One of Nature's greatest gifts is her endless willingness to teach us about our possibilities and ourselves. Through sacred silence we experience the wonders and beauty of animals more intimately, and we begin to realize that every creature mirrors the magnificence of our own soul.

Appendix

Birds	**Quick Reference Guide and Meaning**
Albatross	Be alert for signs of approaching opportunities
Bittern	Heed promises to you
Blackbird	Find a new perspective of the power of nature
Black vulture	Time of transformation is approaching
Bluebird	Good luck and happiness coming in your endeavors
Blue jay	Use your great talent and power properly
Bob white	Time to protect your secrets
Burrowing owl	Stay grounded while working with spirits
Canary	Trust in the power of your voice; work with music
Caracara	Use the available resources
Cardinal	Increase in your vitality and sexuality is coming
Catbird	Be careful of how you communicate
Chickadee	Be truthful and make sure others are as well
Chicken	Time of fertility; trust in divination
Cock (rooster)	Time of increased fertility and resurrection
Cockatoo	Strengthen your relationship bonds
Condor	Time of great protection and spirit contact
Conure	Attend to the family and young around you
Cormorant	Dive deeper for answers and solutions
Cowbird	Resolve family relationships and problems
Crane	Spiritual justice is at play
Crow	Magic is calling and all about you
Cuckoo	A new fate is unfolding and calling
Dove	Time of peace and prophecy
Duck	Seek out emotional comfort
Eagle	Time of great healing and spirit contact
Emu	Fulfill responsibilities while you explore possibilities
Finch	Greater opportunities, activity and potentials awakening
Flamingo	Time to heal the heart
Flicker	New beginnings are near
Goldfinch	Increased contact with spirits and nature
Goose	Heed the call to the new quest
Grackle	Clear out the emotional congestion
Great blue heron	Assert your authority and strike while you can
Grebe	Need for a more creative environment
Grosbeak	Improvement in family matters
Grouse	A time of new sacred rhythms is at hand
Gulls	Watch how you behave and communicate
Gyrfalcon	Maintain a knightly code in your activities
Harrier hawk	Stay grounded while among new spirit and psychic energies
Harris hawk	Cooperate with others for greater success
Hawk	Spirit vision and guardianship around you
Heron	Act with self-reliance
Hummingbird	Opportunity for great joy and accomplishment

Ibis	Healing, magic and protection around you
Kestrel	Act with speed and grace
Killdeer	Guard your creative activities
Kingfisher	New sunshine and prosperity coming
Kite	Need to be adaptable and flexible
Lark	Connections to the ancient bardic tradition opening
Long-eared owl	Be silent but assertive
Loon	Pay attention to the important dream activity
Macaw	Trust your sharp vision and spirit perception
Magpie	Use magic and knowledge properly
Martin	Time of good luck or a change in your fortune
Meadowlark	Find joy within yourself rather than outside of you
Merlin	Time for magical maneuverings
Mockingbird	Look for new opportunities on your path
Night hawk (swisher)	Be diligent and persist
Nuthatch	Have faith but not blind faith in others
Oriole	New sunshine coming
Osprey	Assert new efforts; check your commitments
Ostrich	Be practical & grounded with the new knowledge
Owl	Magic is at play; Pay attention to your dreams
Parakeet	Messages from spirit are at hand
Parrot	Develop and use power of speech for success
Peacock	Protection through psychic / clairvoyant perceptions
Pelican	Time for unselfishness; don't be overcome with emotions
Penguin	Time of lucid dreams and astral projections
Pheasant	Time of fertility and success
Pigeon	Seek security around the home
Puffin	Time for prayer and a sense of humor
Quail	Protection and success through group activities
Raven	Awakening of magic; situations shapeshifting
Roadrunner	Stimulate the mind; act quickly
Robin	Trust in your new creative ideas
Sandhill crane	Time to participate in the dance of life
Sapsucker	Seek out sweetness beneath the surface
Short-eared owl	Carefully develop and use your skills
Secretary bird	Use what you have & do what is best for you
Sharp-shinned hawk	Be prepared to act when opportunity appears
Sparrow	Maintain your dignity and pride
Starling	Time for proper behavior and communication
Stork	Focus your movements for best success
Swallow	Keep objectivity; protect your environment
Swan	Trust in your heart, your true self and your creativity
Swift	Act now in pursuit of your quest
Tufted titmouse	Maintain your dignity and your inner nobility
Turkey	Blessings and abundance are present
Vulture	A time of rebirth and renewed health
Waxwing	Time for gentleness and sharing
White crane	Spiritual justice for you is at play
Woodpecker	Time of new rhythms and new beginnings
Wren	Be resourceful and use what is available

Mammals	**Quick Reference Guide and Meaning**
Aardvark	Your answers lie beneath the surface
Antelope	Time for quick thinking and adaptability
Ape	Be creative in your communications and expressions
Arctic fox	Changes coming with the change of seasons
Armadillo	Use discrimination and protect yourself
Ass (donkey)	Be wise but humble in your new opportunity
Baboon	Maintain groundedness and your sacred space
Badger	Dig beneath the surface for answers; Need to be self-reliant
Bat	Time for change and for new perspectives
Bear	Time to bring out your inner strength explore potentials
Beaver	Time to build toward your dreams
Beluga	Great creativity and new dimensions are opening
Bison	Abundance awaits if you act with respect and honor
Boar	Draw on the family strength and fidelity
Bobcat	Strength and success comes through silence
Bull	Fertile time approaches if we are not too stubborn
Camel	Survival promised through difficult journeys
Capybara	Find refuge in spiritual activities
Caribou	Movement and travel is necessary now
Cat	Mystery and magic is afoot
Cheetah	Time to act with speed and flexibility
Chimpanzee	Be innovative and use new tools
Chipmunk	Balance work and play to enjoy treasures of the earth
Cougar	You are coming into your power; time to assert yourself
Cow	Time of fertility and new birth
Coyote	Balance wisdom and folly in your new endeavors
Deer	Move gently into new areas
Dingo	Be relentless in order to succeed
Dog	Be faithful and alert to protect endeavors
Dolphin	Use the creative power of communication
Eland	Pay attention; divine spirit messages are about
Elephant	Awakening of past life knowledge and ancient power
Elk	Do what must be done; strength and stamina are key
Ferret	New agility in protecting and uncovering secrets
Fox	Situations shifting; magic afoot; do not reveal too much
Gazelle	Trust your intuition and act quickly
Gibbon	Maintain close family ties
Giraffe	Look ahead; be alert to what is coming
Goat	Seek new heights buy be careful of steps
Gorilla	Trust in your inner strength and nobility
Hedgehog	Follow your curiosity
Hippopotamus	Act on your creative ideas; sacred energies awakening
Horse	Trust your intuition in new travels and endeavors
Humpback whale	Time for a new birth in your life
Hyena	Your instincts are strong and formidable – trust them
Impala	Do not hesitate to make new leaps
Jackal	Time of guidance and protection in new realms and endeavors
Jaguar	Time to reclaim your power and the fruits of your labors

Kangaroo	Time to move forward, not back
Koala	Time to calm down, relax and detoxify your life
Lemur	Clairaudience and spirit contact increasing
Lion	Intuition is working; success in group situations
Llama	Balance stubbornness and caution in new endeavors
Lynx	Trust in what you see and feel might be hidden
Manatee	Examine your trust in others doing the right thing
Mole	Time of luck in endeavors through your own efforts
Moose	New birth of power is coming
Mouse	Focus on the details; work on little things
Musk ox	Protection in groups; draw on ancient power
Muskrat	Time to maneuver through emotions and new spiritual waters
Opossum	Be careful of appearances; divert attention
Orangutan	Find new & clever uses for what is available
Otter	Time to use your creativity and your skills together
Panda bear	Combine gentleness with strength for success
Panther	Reclaim what is rightfully yours
Polar bear	Time of great teachings and supernatural power
Porcupine	Balance work and play; keep wonder alive
Prairie dog	Examine your social activity and community involvement
Rabbit	Pay attention to cycles and rhythms; new opportunities
Raccoon	Time of transformation through putting on a proper mask
Ram	Make necessary sacrifices for successful new beginnings
Rat	Be resourceful and shrewd for greatest success
Rhinoceros	Time to put your life in perspective; trust your own wisdom
Sea lion	Time to apply your imagination to your work
Seal	Trust in your dreams and explore your creativity
Shrew	Watch your energy levels and prepare for tougher times
Siberian tiger	Expect an expansion of your power and sensibilities
Skunk	Time to assert your boundaries
Snow leopard	Opportunity to face your fears and demons with success
Squirrel	Balance your work and play
Tiger	Assert your power in new endeavors
Walrus	Powerful psychic touch is awakening
Weasel	Be observant; secrets are about
Whale	Blessings of spirit are coming
Wolf	Time of guardianship on new paths is beginning
Wolverine	Persist and do not surrender
Zebra	Agility – not strength – will bring success now

Insects & Arachnids	**Quick Reference Guide and Meaning**
Ant	Pursue work for the common good
Bee	Time of fertility and strong sexuality
Beetle	Time for resurrection and change
Black & yellow argiope	Time for new perspectives; new dimensions opening
Black widow spider	New fate being woven; chemistry is changing
Butterfly	New love and joy coming
Caterpillar	Good luck and new birth at hand
Centipede	New psychic energies and environments opening
Cicada	Happiness from your past is returning
Cockroach	Be adaptable and sensitive to subtle changes
Cricket	Power of your beliefs is strong – for good or bad
Daddy Longlegs	Time to weave a deeper relationship
Dragonfly	Trust in the power of light
Earthworm	Work through things carefully; cast of what not beneficial
Firefly	Keep hope strong; new inspiration awakening
Flea	Irritations increase until necessary change is made
Grasshopper	New leaps of happiness coming
Jumping spider	Safe time to leap upon new opportunities
Ladybug	Wish will be fulfilled soon
Leech	Time to cleanse and allow joy to flow
Millipede	Psychic sensitivity increases; clairvoyant dreams strong
Mosquito	Protect yourself against attacks on your self-worth
Moth	New relationship or increased sexual energies/activities
Orb weaver spider	Begin to weave / engineer your creative ideas
Praying mantis	Be still and patient for success
Scorpion	Time for transformation
Silkworm moth	Enjoy a time of success and fulfillment
Slug	No shortcuts now; illumination is at hand
Snail	Protect your vulnerable emotions and spirit
Spider	Don't take the round about way; weave something new
Stick bug	Be patient; activity beneath the surface
Tarantula	Change through greater psychic sensitivity
Tick	Relationship(s) unbalanced
Wasp	Protection; dreams fulfilled through practical efforts
Water spider	Pay attention to your dreams
Wolf spider	Assert and pursue your opportunities
Woolly caterpillar	Change of climate is coming to your life

Reptiles & Amphibians	Quick reference Guide and Meaning
Alligator	Act on opportunities for new birth or new knowledge
Basilisk	Dragon guardianship is about you
Boa constrictor	hold tight to what is yours; be true to yourself
Box turtle	Do not rush; you will move through pressures
Chameleon	Clairvoyance is strong; be alert to changing environment
Cobra	Time to make swift and sudden decisions
Copperhead	Do not give in; assert changes
Corn snake	Time of easier movement is at hand
Cottonmouth	Spiritual initiation is at hand; face your fears
Crocodile	Draw on your own instincts and creativity
Frog	Time of coming into your own power; transformation
Garter Snake	Act on as many ideas as possible
Gecko	Do what must be done in struggles
Gila monster	Maintain control; trust in your beliefs
Green anole	Time of harmony and peace is near
Horned lizard	Express your emotions
Iguana	Time to simplify; climb for new goals
Komodo dragon	Trust in your survival instincts and perceptions
Lizard	Pay attention to dreams and psychic perceptions
Milk snake	Be more secretive about intentions and activities
Newt	Time of creative inspirations, ideas & endeavors
Painted turtle	Efforts and faith about to be rewarded
Python	Be patient; incubate your ideas a bit more
Rat snake	Acceleration and movement in all affairs
Rattlesnake	Time of healing and transformation
Salamander	Psychic sensitivity strong; unexpected assistance coming
Sea turtle	Persevere and great success will come
Snake	Time to shed the old; new birth
Snapping turtle	Approach with wariness; be careful of your words
Tadpole	Change is coming; opportunities for new birth/abundance
Toad	Advantage is yours; use skills and resources available
Tortoise	Pressures are easing; movement slow but steady
Tuatara	Slow down; be patient until the time is right
Turtle	Take your time in your pursuits

Sea Life	Quick Reference Guide and Meaning
Angelfish	Unexpected assistance; opportunity for guardianship
Barracuda	Time to go your own way; follow your own path
Bass	Balance opposites and extremes
Carp	Opportunities for achievement on the horizon
Catfish	Your words have great impact; be discerning
Clam	Examine relationship(s); sexual energies strong
Coral	Protection and expansion of family (work or personal)
Crab	Examine issues of sensitivity and reclusiveness
Crayfish	Don't hide from fears; now is the time to try
Damselfish	Show no fear; defend what is yours
Eel	Journey of transformation is ahead
Electric eel	Trust your own perceptions when life is murky
Goldfish	Time of peace and prosperity
Grouper	Disguise what you are doing and feeling
Jellyfish	Coordinate work efforts with others
Moray eel	Time to observe from a safe position; wait for clear opportunity
Mussel	Persevere with endeavors you are attached to
Octopus	Use intelligence, stealth & camouflage to succeed
Salmon	Pilgrimage ahead; persist
Sea Anemone	New tides of wonder coming; go slowly
Sea horse	Time for chivalrous behavior
Shark	Senses heightened; use relentless ferocity in pursuits/defense
Squid	Pay attention to body language of others rather than their words
Starfish	Follow your own unique path
Stingray	Trust in your own inner guidance; stay on course

Bibliography

Andrews, Ted. *Animal-Speak.* St. Paul: Llewellyn Publications, 1993.
__________. Animal-Wise. Jackson, TN: Dragonhawk Publishing,1999.
__________. *Discover Your Spirit Animal (audiocassette).* Dayton, OH: Life Magic Enterprises, Inc., 1996.
__________. *Magical Dance.* St. Paul: Llewellyn Publications, 1992.
__________. *The Animal-Wise Tarot.* Jackson, TN: Dragonhawk Publishing, 1999.

Arnott, Kathleen. *African Myths and Legends.* New York: Oxford University Press, 1989.

Benyus, Janine. *Beastly Behaviors.*New York: Addison-Wesley, 1992.

Caduto, Michael and Bruchac, Joseph. *Keepers of the animals.* Golden, CO: Fulcrum Publishing, 1991.
__________. *Keepers of the Earth.* Golden, CO: Fulcrum Publishing, 1988.

Campbell, Joseph. *The Way of the Animals,* Vol. I & II. New York: Harper & Row, 1988.
__________. *Mythologies of the Primitive Hunters and Gatherers.* New York: Harper & Row, 1988.

Carrier, Jim and Bekoff, Marc. *Nature's Life Lessons.* Golden: Fulcrum Publishing,1996.

Cornell, Joseph. *Sharing Nature with Children.* Nevada City: Dawn Publications, 1979.

Christa, Anthony. *Chinese Mythology.* New York: Peter Bedrick Books, 1983.

Cirlot, J.E. *Dictionary of Symbols.* New York: Philosophical Library, 1962.

Doore, Gary. *The Shaman's Path.* Boston: Shambhala Press, 1988.

Edroes, Richard and Ortiz, Alfonso. *American Indian Myths and Legends.* New York: Pantheon Books, 1984.

Harlow, Rosie and Morgan, Gareth. *175 Amazing Nature Experiements.* New York: Random House, 1991.

Malin, Edward. A World of Faces. Portland: Timber Press,1978.

Palmer, John. *Exploring the Secrets of Nature.* New York: Reader's Digest, 1994.

Rezendes, Paul. *Tracking and the Art of Seeing.* Charlotte, VT: Camden House Pub., 1992.

Smith. Penelope. *Animal Talk.*Hillsboro, OR: Beyond Words Publishing, 1999.

Tanner, Ogden. *Urban Wilds.* Alexandria: Time-Life Books, 1975.

Index

G

H

I

J

K

L

M

N

O

P

R

S

T

W

Y

Margaret K. Andrews

About the Author

Ted Andrews (1952-2009) was an award-winning author and deeply respected teacher in the metaphysical and spiritual fields. Through his seminars, symposiums, workshops, and lectures, he was committed to making esoteric material comprehensible and practical for everyone.

Ted Andrews's many gifts included clairvoyancy, aura interpretation, past-life analysis, dreams interpretation, numerology, and Tarot. He wrote many books on these subjects, but is best known for his work with animal mysticism. Certified in basic hypnosis and acupressure, Andrews was also involved in the study and use of herbs as an alternative path in health care, focusing strongly on esoteric forms of healing with sound, music, and voice. In addition to his interest in metaphysics, Ted was a trained pianist and often used the Celtic harp, bamboo flute, shaman rattles, Tibetan bells, Tibetan Singing Bowl, and quartz crystal bowls to create individual healing therapies and induce higher states of consciousness.

Ted Andrews is the author of *The Healer's Manual;* Animal-Speak; *How to See & Read the Aura; Enchantment of the Faerie Realm; Crystal Balls & Crystal Bowls; How to Uncover Your Past Lives; How to Heal with Color; Sacred Sounds; Simplified Qabala Magic;* and many other New Age titles. He passed away on October 24, 2009.

Roxanna Walitzki

About the Artist

Siolo Thompson (Seattle, WA) is a visual artist and author who employs multiple techniques and narrative forms, from traditional painting to comics and sequential illustration. Her work has been published and exhibited worldwide. She is the creator of *The Linestrider Tarot, Otherkin Tarot, Hedgewitch Botanical Oracle, Winterseer Animal Oracle, Seaborn Kipper,* and more. Visit her at SioloThompson.com.